# Weekend Life Coach

## How to get the life you want in 48 hours

## Lynda Field

**Vermilion**
LONDON

First published in 2004 by Vermilion,
an imprint of Ebury Press, Random House,
20 Vauxhall Bridge Road, London SW1V 2SA

Random House Australia (Pty) Limited
20 Alfred Street, Milsons Point, Sydney,
New South Wales 2061, Australia

Random House New Zealand Limited
18 Poland Road, Glenfield,
Auckland 10, New Zealand

Random House South Africa (Pty) Limited
Endulini, 5A Jubilee Road,
Parktown 2193, South Africa

The Random House Group Limited Reg. No. 954009

Papers used by Rider are natural, recyclable products made from wood grown
in sustainable forests.

Printed and bound by Mackays of Chatham Ltd, Chatham, Kent
A CIP catalogue record for this book
is available from the British Library

ISBN 0-09-189468-9

# Contents

## Part One:
## SEVEN STEPS TO BEING YOUR OWN LIFE COACH

## Part Two:
## GET THE LIFE YOU WANT

*This book is dedicated to my husband, Richard Field, with my utmost gratitude and love.*

# Acknowledgements

THANK YOU

To my wonderful family, who remind me that love is the greatest gift.

To my friends, who are always there for me, especially Sue Roberts and Barbara Higham.

To my clients and colleagues, who remind me that there is always a new book to be written.

To the fabulous team at Ebury Press, who have worked so hard to bring this book into being; I appreciate all your support. And extra special thanks to Judith Kendra, my brilliant editor (patient as a saint!), and also the multi-talented Caroline Newbury, who is *always* cheerful and optimistic.

# Preface
## Your Dreams Can Come True

*If you only care enough for a result, you will almost certainly attain it.*

WILLIAM JAMES

My job is to help people change for the better. In the last 20 years I have done this by writing books, giving one-to-one counselling, running courses and workshops, and life coaching. Over the years my clients have taught me something of vital importance: positive changes always happen when we are focused and relaxed, and never when we are stressed and rushed. When we are tense and uptight there is no time or space to embrace new ways of being in the world; it can sometimes feel as if we have to keep running at top speed just to stay in the same place. Although most people would like to make changes in their lives, many feel that they just don't have the time to think clearly about their problem areas, let alone to begin to sort them out. If you have ever felt too stretched and stressed to get a grip on your life, *Weekend Life Coach* is for you.

The best time for most of us to find some space for ourselves is at the weekend, when we are feeling less rushed. So why not make next weekend an opportunity to relax, refocus and take a fresh look at your life.

Change can happen surprisingly quickly. As soon as you believe in yourself and your capacity to move forward (in whatever area of your life), the changes you want can start right away. This book will help you to create all the self-confidence and self-belief that you need to turn your life around. You can do anything when you believe that you can!

Experience has shown me that a calm and relaxed approach to life coaching can rapidly bring results, and that self-transformation can be fascinating and fun. In fact, the greater your enjoyment, the more notable will be your success. And so this book is designed to inspire and empower you in a relaxed yet focused way. Yes, there will be issues to think about, emotions to reflect upon and actions to take, but all my tips, strategies and techniques are easy and enjoyable to use. They are very effective and have been well tried and tested by my clients.

*Weekend Life Coach* looks at all aspects of your life, including how to be confident, have brilliant relationships, do the work you love, feel calm and peaceful, get more energy, unwind and de-stress, attract success, control your weight, and look and feel fantastic. Your dreams can come true. You only have to make a commitment to taking the next step and your wonderful new life will unfold before your very eyes. What are you waiting for? Let us begin!

# Introduction
## Go For It!

*An ounce of action is worth a ton*
*of theory.*

FRIEDRICH ENGELS

You can be whatever you want to be. There is absolutely no
doubt about the truth of this statement, though sometimes you
might find it difficult to believe. Life is too short to stuff a
mushroom and also too short to waste in hanging back, under-
selling yourself and being less than your best. Imagine yourself
in ten years time: where would you like to be, with whom and
doing what? Are you working towards these goals right now or
are they just your wishes and hopes for the future? If your
dreams feel far away or somewhat unrealistic, you can bring
them into your reality right now, in this very moment, by
making a commitment to yourself to change your life.

I wrote this book for you, to provide the simple guidelines
that you need to be whatever you want to be and to do
whatever you want to do. My job is to show you how you *can*
live your dreams and become the star in the performance of
your life. And your job is to make a commitment to yourself to
undergo the coaching process and to be ready to embrace the
new. At the end of this introduction there is a contract for
you to sign, so confirming this promise to yourself. Your

commitment to change is a magic key to unlocking the energy that you need to achieve your goals.

I have worked with hundreds of people from all walks of life. At one stage, when I was living in Cornwall, I spent weekdays motivating and career counselling disaffected teenagers and then went to London at the weekend to run motivational courses for TV executives. Now you might think that these two groups of people had very different needs, but I discovered something very interesting: you can be well educated with a high-powered and glamorous job and still lack the confidence to be yourself, and you can be an unemployed youngster with learning difficulties and still be highly motivated to find your place in the world. My experience of coaching has shown me that everyone (whatever their circumstances) can take charge of their life and turn themselves around *as long as they believe in themselves*. Self-belief gives you energy, focus and confidence, and lies at the very heart of successful self-change.

## How to use this book

A restful weekend is a perfect time to concentrate on yourself and your needs. Yes, you will always have chores to do – shopping to get, cleaning to do, washing to sort... Just reschedule them! Plan the free time you will need to work with me to change your life. Prioritise yourself – your life is waiting!

And when you have found the time, why not create a peaceful haven for yourself, wherever you are? You might like to listen to your favourite background music, put your feet up or burn some relaxing aromatherapy oils. Really get into the mood of the moment. Start at the beginning and work your way through the book and have a notebook and pen handy to jot down any thoughts or reflections.

Throughout *Weekend Life Coach* you will find Quick Tips that offer instant ways to make positive changes *fast*. And every chapter contains Time Outs to keep your mood calm, stress-free and upbeat. So you can remain motivated and focused all weekend and also stay relaxed and centred.

Part One of this book is a simple guide to taking control of your life.

**Step 1:** Reach For Your Best shows you how to use your thoughts, beliefs and expectations to create a winning mentality. You can attract success and be your best in any area of your life if you just decide to change your state of mind.

**Step 2:** Get Focused invites you to take a realistic look at where you are right now and where you really want to be. It then shows you how by changing your vision of yourself you can create new and vibrant goals.

**Step 3:** Keep Motivated explains how developing confidence and high self-esteem will enable you to stay positive and empowered. With strong self-belief you can achieve anything!

**Step 4:** Transform Negative Energy explains how self-doubt holds us back and makes us fearful of change. With an open heart and mind you can learn to change any negative state into a positive one. Your new assertive communication skills will transform your relationships and give you the strength and optimism to step into the new.

**Step 5:** Be Inspired reminds you that you are a shining star and your life is full of meaning and purpose. As you connect with the universal life force, you develop the skills of intuition, telepathy and deep awareness. When you are feeling inspired you really are going with the flow, and it's a fabulous feeling of excitement and exhilaration. Yes, being happy leads to great things!

**Step 6** Act Now lays it on the line: no more ifs and buts, the time is now! Procrastination and time-wasting are guilt-inducing activities that sap your energy. Action speaks louder than words, and by now you will know exactly what you need to do. Be decisive, take positive steps and move into your own power.

**Step 7:** Take Control shows you how to get organised and make your time work for you. Take the pressure off by streamlining your life and making the best use of your time. Efficient planning can lead to great success and the achievement of all your goals.

Whenever you need support or guidance just look back over these seven steps. If you are feeling blocked and stuck in any area of your life, you are not taking one or more of the steps. So let them become part of your personal mantra for creating success and being happy. When the going gets tough, know that there is some energy that needs shifting and ask yourself the following questions:

- Am I reaching for my best?
- Do I know where I am and where I want to be?
- Am I feeling motivated and do I believe in myself?
- Am I transforming negative energy or am I being dragged into pessimism?
- Do I feel inspired and in the flow?
- Have I begun to take action, or am I still holding back?
- Am I in control?

Use the simple strategies, tools and techniques in Part One of this book to empower you to become your own life coach and to make the changes you desire. Only you can really know yourself; only you will always be there through your personal ups and downs. So find out exactly how you tick, what works for you and what doesn't, what keeps you positive and upbeat, what you do to overcome obstacles and challenges and still keep smiling. Your life is an amazing adventure, so discover how to get enthusiastic about your future and generate some real excitement – you have everything to gain. And don't be shy about your strengths and talents; learn to become your biggest fan, because self-belief is pure magic!

Part Two of the book concentrates on the six issues that are top of the 'need to change' list for most of my clients:

- confidence
- weight
- happiness
- career
- relationships
- money

It shows you how the super-confident new you can get real results in each of these areas.

You always have the power to create new, exciting opportunities for yourself, and your life will immediately become richer and more fascinating when you are ready to go out and meet it. Decide to go for it! Sign and date your commitment contract and step into your new life, right now!

# MY CONTRACT

I . . . . . . . . . . . . . . . . . . . . . . . . . . . . .

commit myself to finding the time I need to read
this book. I am ready to make changes and
I honour my decision to reach for my best.

I agree to do the exercises and use the
strategies and really focus on improving my life.

I am determined to succeed and I know
that I will.

Signature: . . . . . . . . . . . . . . . . . . . . . . . . . . .

Date: . . . . . . . . . . . . . . . . . . . . . . . . . . . . .

# Part One

# SEVEN STEPS TO BEING YOUR OWN LIFE COACH

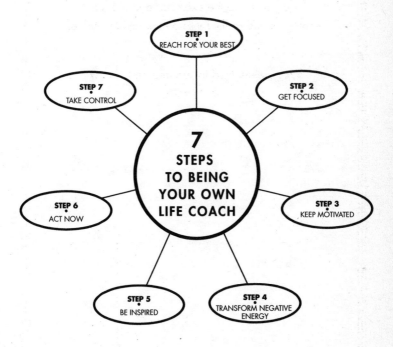

# Step 1
# Reach for Your Best

*You must do the thing*
*you think you cannot do.*

ELEANOR ROOSEVELT

When you walk into a room you take with you all that you are. You carry with you an intangible 'beingness' that everyone can sense at the very deepest level. Although you may have checked yourself in the mirror beforehand – hair, makeup, clothes, shoes – you will have seen only the external part of your image. Personal presentation is important but it means nothing if you don't have inner style.

For a recent *Cosmopolitan* makeover feature I worked as a confidence coach, alongside the stylist and hair and beauty experts, to create a total change of image for three readers. While fabulous clothes, beautiful hair and flattering makeup can do wonders for our ego, we also need that inner confidence to feel totally relaxed and fabulous. Many of us are beginning to recognise that what we feel inside has a great influence on how we operate out in the world.

## Success attracts success

This sense of beingness is an expression of yourself that depends entirely on your thoughts, beliefs and expectations. And it tells others a huge amount about you. If you are self-confident it shows in your body language, in your face and in the very words that you use. And if you are struggling with self-doubt and insecurity this shows too. We draw to ourselves the experiences that fulfil our beliefs and expectations. These self-fulfilling prophecies work like this:

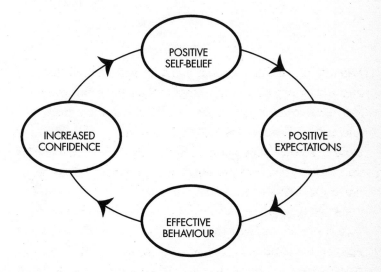

**POSITIVE SELF-FULFILLING PROPHECY**

Cast your mind back to a time when you were feeling really great. Can you see how your positive inner feelings helped you to create a good outcome, which only reinforced your feelings of self-worth?

And now let's look at the negative cycle:

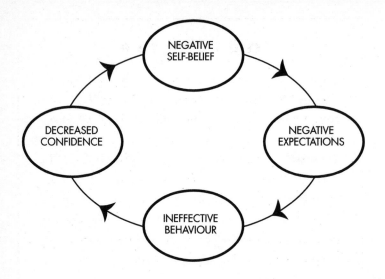

**NEGATIVE SELF-FULFILLING PROPHECY**

Now think of a time when you were going through this cycle. Remember how easy it was to go down. And believe me, we can all go down if we let ourselves! Don't go there! Recognise that negativity attracts more of the same and be ready to root it out at all times.

Knowledge is power, so get to know whatever it is that you cling to that doesn't work for you any more. When you know what is holding you back you can let go and move on; this is the way to create success for yourself. Adopt this positive attitude to your own growth process. As you develop the heightened sense of self-awareness that working through this book will bring you, learn to use *all* your self-knowledge to your best advantage. In this way *everything* that you think, feel and do will help you to understand where you are going and why, and how you can open the doors to new and exciting possibilities. You may be surprised to discover that your significant turning points have often come during a particularly challenging phase in which your nerve is severely tested. When you survive such a test you become stronger and more resolute and realise that you are indeed made of powerful stuff.

## Be a winner

*Winning isn't always about being number one – winning is a state of mind.*

ZOE KOPLOWITZ

There's winning and there's winning. There's being best and coming first, and then there's being the best you can be whatever your situation.

I first heard about Zoe Koplowitz in 1999, when I read a

small piece in a newspaper about her remarkable achievement. A 50-year-old American, who was a diabetic and a multiple sclerosis sufferer, she had just crossed the finishing line of the London Marathon. Zoe completed the 26-mile race on a pair of purple crutches, and it took her 30 hours – 28 more than the winner.

When I began writing this chapter I remembered Zoe and searched the Internet to see what she is up to these days. And what do you think? She has gone from strength to strength and is now proud to hold the distinction of being the world's slowest marathon runner. She has become famous in the USA, having gone on to complete 13 consecutive 26.2-mile New York marathons, raise extensive funds for the MS Society and write an inspiring book called *Winning Spirit*. Zoe says she thinks her runs have attracted so much media attention, because 'the trend is finally turning from 'being first is best' to 'being the best you can be'.

What a fabulous story. We can be uplifted by hearing about others who have shown amazing courage and resilience; we can share their strength and be reminded that human beings are magnificently powerful. Let this feeling inspire you to step into your own potential. You are bigger than you think you are!

## You have what it takes

How do I know that you have hidden potential? Why do I think I can help you to get the best out of yourself?

I believe that you are filled with unlimited personal power and that, given positive support and simple guidelines, you can reach into yourself and allow your natural talents and strengths to blossom. We all know examples of people who have surpassed all expectations of themselves when faced with

## TIME OUT

PUT YOUR BOOK DOWN AND TAKE A FEW MOMENTS TO RELAX. LOOK AROUND YOU AND THINK ABOUT THE TRUE MIRACLE OF YOUR LIFE. MAYBE YOU CAN SEE THE CLOUDS OUT OF YOUR WINDOW. WHY NOT INDULGE IN A SPOT OF CLOUD-WATCHING? DO NOTHING OTHER THAN WATCH THE CLOUDS AND LET GO OF ALL YOUR PREOCCUPATIONS. ENJOY BEING HERE IN THIS MOMENT, BREATHING AND APPRECIATING THE BEAUTY OF THE NATURAL WORLD. TAKE TIME TO ENJOY YOUR MOMENTS. THIS WILL ALWAYS STRENGTHEN AND SUSTAIN YOU. CLOUD-WATCHING IS AN ACTIVITY WITH NO OTHER PURPOSE THAN TO HELP YOU APPRECIATE THE PRECIOUSNESS OF YOUR LIFE. YOUR LIFE IS PRECIOUS AND SO ARE YOU!

a crisis. People just like you and me can really pull out the stops when we have to.

In extreme situations we are urgently required to dig deep into ourselves, to find new and greater personal strengths to meet our challenges. And because we need more resources we find them – hence the opportunity to grow that a crisis brings. But why wait for disaster to strike before you reach for your hidden skills and underused abilities? If your life is not to your liking, don't sit around waiting for it to change. Why hang around until you get the sack from your boring job before you make that great new career move? Why stay in a poor relationship when there are so many fish in the sea? And if you are feeling stressed and overstretched, slow down, take a fresh look at where you are going and why, before you burn out.

Life's winners are people who have decided that the words 'average', 'normal', 'usual' and 'predictable' do not necessarily apply to them. To live an extraordinary life you *must* be ready to become bigger than ordinary. This may mean that you don't always stick to convention and it will certainly mean being ready to be your absolutely unique and original self.

Think of the people who stand out in life; they are unusual in the sense that they have an added charisma and style that jet-propels them to success. This personal magnetism acts like a high-octane fuel to create winners, optimists and positive thinkers. Creative and powerful entrepreneurs such as Anita Roddick and Richard Branson spring to mind – people who have used all their skills and focus to create something much more than a great business. Then, in the media world, we have Steven Spielberg directing brilliant movies with powerful messages and Madonna, who goes on reinventing herself to perfection. Sporting heroes like Tiger Woods and the Williams sisters are great examples of winners who use all the tips and techniques of positive thinking and visualisation to create their outcomes. Extend this list of successful and motivated people and you will notice that all of them have a strong sense of self and purpose. I'm not suggesting that you need to be an A-list celebrity to be a winner, not at all. But to have got where they are *and to have stayed there* these people have had to reach continually for the very best within themselves and have maintained 100 per cent belief in their goals. Just think how your life would change if you kept reaching for your best!

Next time you are sitting on a train or bus or even walking down a street, take a close look at the people around you. Notice their energy (you can see and feel this very easily). Are they light and optimistic? Do they look happy and alert? Are they glowing with interest? Do they have a spark? Do they meet your eyes when you glance at them?

You will see that the majority of people are preoccupied with their thoughts, and by the look of them these thoughts are not very optimistic. And here lies a vital point: positive people get the results they want because they believe in themselves and they believe in life. You have the power to turn around any negative state of mind and this will unlock your amazing creative potential. Are you ready to stand out and be different from the mainstream? Are you ready to attract success?

## 10 Ways to attract success

1 Be true to yourself.
2 Celebrate your uniqueness – this is what makes you special.
3 Develop your inner strengths and talents.
4 Think big.
5 Believe in yourself and radiate confidence.
6 Take the first step towards one of your goals.
7 Appreciate the miracle of your life.
8 Love and value all your experiences.
9 Be a go-getter.
10 Never, ever give up!

## Mind power

There is an old story that tells of a traveller who met a wise man at the walls of a city.

'What sort of people live here?' enquired the traveller.

The sage replied, 'What are the people like where you have come from?'

'Oh they are thoughtless, bigoted and hypocritical,' replied the traveller.

'That is just how you will find the people here,' said the sage.

Some time later another wanderer approached the wise man and asked, 'Can you tell me what the people are like who live within these walls?'

The sage said, 'Tell me what the people are like where you come from.'

'Why, they are kind and generous and everyone looks out for each other,' the traveller replied.

'Well, that is just how you will find the people here,' declared the sage.

The thoughts you have, the words you speak and the pictures that you carry in your mind create the reality that you experience. Negative thoughts and visions will not draw the positive changes that you are looking for; positive energy will!

When you were tiny you learned how to feel about yourself and your world through the speech and actions of the adults in your life. Your enquiring and totally trusting mind was like a sponge that mopped up everything in its path, whether it was positive, negative, frightening, supportive, threatening, loving or whatever. As a baby and small child you unquestioningly absorbed and believed all the messages that were relayed in your environment. They may have been spoken messages or they may have been more subtle thought and behaviour patterns that influenced your home life. You internalised these messages and made them part of your own belief system. In this way you have unconsciously programmed your mind so that you act, feel and behave in certain prescribed ways. So your mental, emotional and behavioural patterns are just habits that you have learned! Your beliefs aren't carved in stone and if they don't work for you then you can change them. We will look at how our programming affects our lives later in the book, but for now just recognise that you see the world through the filter of your learned perceptions.

If we believe and expect that others are hostile and unfriendly then we will soon prove this to be true (as we approach others warily and with suspicion). But if we believe in the intrinsic goodness of our fellow humans our trust will attract the best in people (as they rise to fulfil our expectations). It's not *what* you see but *how* you see that makes the difference. Once you understand the ways that your negative patterns can limit your life, you possess the most wonderful piece of knowledge: you can change your negative patterns into positive patterns. This means that you have the power to remove all those self-imposed limitations and be free to become your best self.

## EXERCISE:

# Recognise negative and positive patterns

Scientific research at the University of California has proved that the more we reinforce a pattern by repeating it, the more powerful it becomes and that if we stop using a pattern, it will become weaker and weaker. So start to develop your own negativity and positivity awareness. You can do this in two ways:

1 Listen to others and start to really hear their negative and positive words and phrases (it's probably best to keep the

nature of your research to yourself). Just start noticing and in a very short time you will become increasingly aware of the difference between positive and negative energy.

**2** Listen to yourself, your words and your thoughts. No need to become self-critical here (this is never a useful tool). Remain as detached as possible as you allow yourself to become conscious of the ways that you demonstrate your positive and negative beliefs.

Reflect upon what you discover. Think about the nature of your personal thought patterns and write down your findings in your notebook. This will be useful to you later.

## Wake up to your life

To reach for your best and attract success you need to develop a talent that you already possess; you need to become more self-aware. When things go wrong and you feel flat, the wonderful transforming powers of self-awareness will always open you up to new levels of experience so that you can gain new insights, raise your game and feel more energetic and alive.

Awareness changes your energy levels. It can come like a bolt from the blue or, less dramatically, the penny might finally drop; either way you will feel the change. Cast your mind back to a time when this happened to you. Maybe you caught yourself making a self-critical comment or negative judgement and you suddenly realised what you were doing. Perhaps some unfinished business from the past reared its head and you recognised the need to deal with it immediately (it couldn't be put off for one moment longer). Or possibly you found yourself seeing someone clearly as if for the first time, and finally understood the true nature of your relationship with them.

Personal insights bring a sense of realisation and amazement and you immediately become more alert and aware (the feeling is one of: *wait a minute, what's going on here?*). As soon as you are ready to wake up to your life and check out the details, you get to see what is really happening and why. When you start to look your life in the eye it gets easier to make the right decisions and take the right action. This reality check will bring you new and powerful energy and suddenly you will be going with the flow instead of swimming against the tide.

Being self-aware does not ever limit your action, but it does mean that whatever you do will be consciously chosen and not result from a purely emotional response. This means the end to all those knee-jerk reactions, which can bring you so much grief. How many times have you lived to regret those angry outbursts or inappropriate comments which just seemed to rise up in you from nowhere in the heat of the moment? Rash responses can turn an intimate relationship into a war zone in a matter of seconds, and who needs this?

Increasing self-awareness brings a new way of looking at your life and your relationships. With this greater understanding you seem to have more time and space to consider your thoughts and feelings; your energy is more expansive and your responses become more creative and effective.

## See more, feel more, be more

Self-awareness is not just a concept; it is a real and practical tool that can enable you to lift your day-to-day experience from the mundane to the fascinating. You get to see more, feel more and be more! There will be times, when the going gets rough, when you will want to abandon this growth process.

Becoming aware requires that you remain open-minded and open-hearted and sometimes this can feel very hard to do. When you are feeling insecure, threatened or criticised, your self-doubt can lead you into a negative cycle in which you start to close down your heart and mind. This may feel like a defensive or protective measure but it really only serves to cut you off from that sense of aliveness and energy that comes when you are aware and conscious of your thoughts, feelings and behaviour. Whenever you choose to close down, your energy level drops, causing you to feel generally 'lower', and your daily life becomes dull and uninspiring.

So let boredom and apathy be danger signals warning you that it's time to wake up to the reality of your life and start to make your day count – right now, in the very moment that you recognise these feelings. Your self-awareness can bring each second fully alive; even those moments of dullness can be used as an alarm bell.

## Encourage yourself

As you get to know more about yourself you will probably discover that *you are not who you thought you were!* You are powerful and brilliant, so why not let your light really shine? No more hiding in the shadows doubting your worth and abilities. Look inside yourself and you will always find all that you need to take your next step.

Getting to know yourself means learning how to be on your own side. I frequently talk about this to my clients. Maybe it's because we often find it hard to take good care of our own interests (although we are usually really good at looking after others!). If you ever start to treat yourself badly by being self-critical and judgemental, you lose trust in yourself and your own abilities.

# Make each day count

Try the following techniques to help you feel fully alive throughout the day.

- Write 'EVERY DAY COUNTS' on a large piece of paper and display it prominently. Make smaller copies for your car/handbag/desk at work. Reminders are always useful – it's so easy to get lost in our personal dramas and forget to stay focused.

- Stay open to new ideas and possibilities; change always involves embracing the new.

- Notice any situations where you start to withdraw your energy. Are you feeling threatened? If so, what is making you feel insecure?

- Don't let emotional impulses run your life; think before you act.

- Relax and give yourself the chance to go with the flow.

- Remember that you are here for a purpose.

- Commit yourself to your life.

---

Think about the great relationship you have with your best friend. You share the good and the bad times with her and are always there with encouragement and support. Why not develop a relationship like this with yourself? Become your own greatest ally and don't ever bring yourself down (in thought, word or deed). Love and honour yourself. You deserve this.

Don't become bogged down in self-criticism; you can free yourself of all the self-limiting beliefs that hold you back. You can be your own worst enemy or your own best friend.

Self-belief gives you the will to reach for your best and win, whatever the circumstances. Know that it is always your inner strength that will win through for you; your biggest challenge will always be yourself. Winners are determined and focused and they can never lose because they always believe in what they are doing. They bounce back and keep on going whatever obstacles they encounter. You have this inner strength and commitment. The past has no power over you; you can make new choices in the present moment – now! Reach for your best.

# TIME OUT

## FIVE-MINUTE RELAXATION

### RELAXING YOUR BODY

SIT OR LIE IN A COMFORTABLE POSITION AND CLOSE YOUR EYES. TAKE A DEEP BREATH AND JUST FEEL THE STRESSES AND STRAINS DROP AWAY. PAY ATTENTION TO THE RHYTHM OF YOUR BREATHING. AS YOU INHALE, IMAGINE THAT YOU ARE BEING FILLED WITH PEACE. AS YOU EXHALE, IMAGINE THAT YOU ARE LETTING GO OF ALL THE TENSIONS IN YOUR BODY.

JUST FOLLOW YOUR BREATH, INHALING PEACE AND EXHALING PHYSICAL TENSION.

### RELAXING YOUR MIND

TAKE ANOTHER DEEP BREATH AND AS YOU INHALE, IMAGINE THAT YOU ARE BEING FILLED WITH PEACE. AS YOU EXHALE, IMAGINE THAT YOU ARE LETTING GO OF ALL YOUR STRESS AND WORRIES.

JUST FOLLOW YOUR BREATH, INHALING PEACE AND EXHALING MENTAL STRESS.

### LETTING EVERYTHING GO

TAKE ANOTHER DEEP BREATH AND RELAX COMPLETELY. AS YOU LET GO, YOU FIND YOURSELF IN A QUIET PLACE, DEEP WITHIN YOU. REST HERE FOR AS LONG AS YOU WISH.

### COMING BACK

WHEN YOU ARE READY, OPEN YOUR EYES AND SLOWLY COME BACK INTO THE ROOM. STAY WITH YOUR RELAXED FEELINGS AS LONG AS YOU CAN.

# Step 2
# Get Focused

*Singleness of purpose is one of the*
*chief essentials for success in life,*
*no matter what may be one's aim.*

JOHN D. ROCKEFELLER JR

Life is full of surprises. Who knows what may be around the next corner? Although it is exciting to live in high expectation, wouldn't it be great to know that your hopes were grounded in strong and real possibility because the odds were always stacked in your favour?

Waiting for 'something' to happen, the hand of fate to intervene, Lady Luck to miraculously appear, will keep you stewing in uncertainty, and this can feel very uncomfortable! It is so much better to know that you have made a conscious choice about where you are going and why; drifting aimlessly is only enjoyable if you are doing it in your relaxation time. I love this Portuguese fishermen's saying: 'Pray to God but pull for the shore'. In other words, having faith is great but you must do your bit. And your bit is easy.

All you have to do is to discover what you want and then do everything in your power to make it happen. This requires both focus and self-awareness. Specify your goals, know your personal strengths and talents, respect your own values and opinions, and then add a dash of your own personal flair! These things together create a potent spell for success.

Whenever I begin a coaching session with a new client I always start by asking them what exactly they want to achieve. They may find it easy to answer, for example: I want to lose weight/get a new job/be more confident in relationships. But if they are feeling stuck or uncertain or that life is just not right or that they don't know which way to turn, answering this question almost always gives them back a sense of power and purpose. Ask yourself: What do I want to happen? Never mind about how; at this stage, having a clear 'what' is the way to develop the focused vision that leads to successful change.

## EXERCISE:

# What about your life?

Answer the following questions:

1  What have you always wanted to do but have been too afraid to try?

2  What would you do differently in your life if money was no object?

3  What do you consider to be your greatest personal strengths?

4  You are living your dreams. What do they look like and how do you feel?

## The Life Wheel

In the following Life Wheel diagram each section represents an area of our life. At the very centre the satisfaction level is 0 (totally dissatisfied) and at the outer edge it is 10 (totally satisfied).

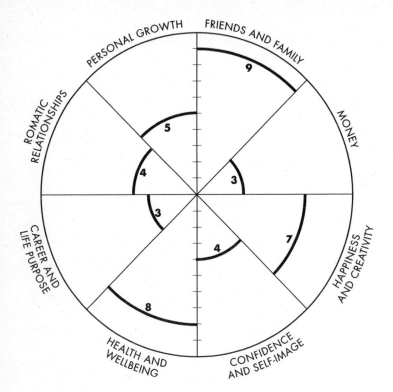

**EXAMPLE OF A LIFE WHEEL**

# Your Life Wheel

Rank your satisfaction levels on your own Life Wheel. Is your life fairly well balanced or does the shape of your Wheel make it an uncomfortable ride? Which areas are you happy with? Where would you like to make changes? We will come back to this diagram later.

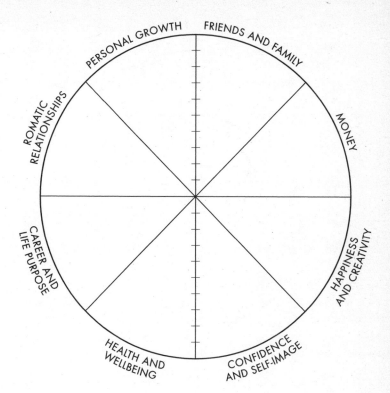

**YOUR LIFE WHEEL**

## The importance of goals

Consider this: if you carry on doing what you are doing, you are going to get the same results.

World famous hypnotist Paul McKenna is a man who walks his talk. He says that his life changed 10 years ago when he sat down and asked himself, 'If I continue along my present course, where will I end up five years from now?' He realised that he wouldn't be any more fulfilled (emotionally, financially or otherwise) and so he asked himself what he really wanted and what was important to him. From that moment he hasn't looked back. He pinpointed his goals and started to visualise them coming true, and they did. Suddenly he was more energetic and enthusiastic and his fortunes took a turn for the better. He went on to become an international star, attracting the attention of media celebrities and royalty. Paul has become a major success in his field because he created a personal goal and kept focused on it. He says, 'If I hadn't identified that goal and worked towards it, I'm sure I wouldn't be where I am today.'

The point is that we all set goals, whether we are aware of it or not. Look at your life today and recognise that whatever you are doing and whoever you are doing it with are direct results of decisions you acted on (or didn't) in the past. Consider three aspects of your life, for example relationships, finances and career. In each area think of a way in which a past decision or action has helped to create something positive in each of these areas. Now think about a way in which your behaviour and decisions helped to create things that you didn't want to happen. Can you see the part you played in creating these outcomes? Once you become conscious of the goal-setting process, you can really go for what you want, and get it!

## The powerhouse of your mind

GIGO is a well known term in the computer world. It stands for 'garbage in, garbage out'. If you programme a computer with garbage, all you can get out is garbage.

The largest and most influential part of the mind is subconscious. The subconscious mind works just like a computer, analysing, computing, plotting, planning and helping you to create whatever it is that you really wish for and dream about. When you look at your life you may be wondering how this can be true! But even as you read this paragraph, your subconscious is busy working away, recognising your main concerns, picking up relevant facts and assimilating and organising them into a surefire plan to achieve your ideal outcomes. This plan will bring you whatever your subconscious is programmed to believe you want. The big question is: what does your subconscious think that you want?

If you are feeding it with negative statements such as 'I am afraid' and 'I never succeed', then your subconscious will loyally work to manifest more of these things for you: it gives you exactly what you ask for. If, on the other hand, you feed it with statements such as 'I am wealthy' and 'My life is happy', it will work to create these expectations. The subconscious mind takes everything literally. Your subconscious is your greatest and most powerful friend; it is always on your side and it will always find ways of proving to you that your beliefs are true.

## Elinor's story

Elinor was a researcher for a television company. I met her when I was promoting a book on a programme she was working on. The book was about confidence and success, and she wanted more of those, so she decided to have some coaching.

She was good at her job and was working towards becoming an assistant producer (and eventually hoped to run her own production company). Elinor was gorgeous, intelligent, funny and really good at her job, but she felt unsure of herself. The media world is very competitive and you really need to have a thick skin to survive, let alone get promoted. Elinor's goal was to go for a new job as assistant producer on an upcoming reality TV show; she had all the skill, experience and ability but was terrified of the interview. She said that at other interviews she had let herself down badly and this had made her lose her nerve even more. She had a dream of a successful promotion but her subconscious kept delivering failure.

I asked Elinor to think about what success meant to her. She wrote 'Success means ...' at the top of the page and then jotted down what came to her. And how interesting it was! Top of the list was not happiness, joy, satisfaction, achievement or any of the things you might expect success to be linked with.

She wrote: 'Success means thinking I'm better than I am, getting too big for my boots, maybe losing my friends, maybe people not liking me any more, not being one of the gang.'

Elinor had been a bright girl on a council estate who had won a scholarship to an Independent school at the age of 11. From the moment she left the local primary she became an outsider, different from the children she had grown up with. As a result, the adult Elinor really wanted to succeed but always had mixed feelings about being chosen as the best.

This is a great example of the power of the subconscious at work. It is possible to have a real dream and to be motivated to realise it but still block your own progress. Elinor soon recognised how she had programmed her subconscious for failure. Her beliefs about success were negative and the pictures in her head linked it with her childhood sense of being different from her old friends and losing their companionship.

Elinor set about reprogramming her subconscious with positive statements and upbeat visualisations about success. She began to link success with doing a good job, having fun and moving on in life. Her self-image changed completely, and I hardly need to tell you that, yes, she got the job!

You can overcome all your personal obstacles by reprogramming your mind. If you programme your subconscious with positive beliefs, images and expectations, then these are what will come true for you.

Try the exercise that I gave Elinor. Imagine that a dream has come true. How does it feel? Write 'Success means ...' at the top of a page in your notebook and without thinking about it too much just brainstorm and write whatever you feel. What you write will be an indication of how close you are to achieving success. If your feelings are positive, you are already on the way; if they are negative, they can be changed. Start living the dream by imagining it happening and see yourself *feeling great*.

## Prepare yourself for success

Before we look in more detail at goal-setting, I want you to prepare yourself for success. Your attitude to yourself and your life will determine what happens to you, so a positive approach is absolutely necessary if you want to achieve your goals.

Good ideas are great, but they will only work if they are put into action, and we tend only to bother to activate the things that really motivate us. You will never do something that you think you 'might like to do' or feel that you 'should do' for some reason. If you are going to reach a goal you have to be delighted and excited by the prospect. Think back to a plan you had that never quite materialised. Ask yourself, 'How much did I want to do that?' The answer will be 'not enough'. Now think of a successfully completed project. I bet that was something you really wanted to do, wasn't it? Don't make half-hearted promises to yourself, because at a deeper level you will know that they are never going to happen. Each time you don't do what you say you are going to do, you will feel worse about yourself, so keep your confidence up by going only for things that thrill you to bits.

Of course, it's much easier to reach a short-term and realistically achievable goal (go and buy that 'must have' designer bag) than it is to go for something that asks for more commitment in time and energy (take up jogging and get fit). The trick here is to break down all your goals into manageable steps. Let your motto be 'One step at a time'. Write it on a piece of brightly coloured card and post it on your fridge or any other prominent place so that it can act as a constant reminder to you. The bigger your desired goal, the longer it will probably take to achieve, so don't let yourself become disillusioned. Just break it down into achievable chunks and recognise and celebrate each successful step along the way.

Roger Bannister was the first man to run the four-minute mile. He trained his body and his mind in a very specific and calculated way. He broke down the mile into four quarters and began by sprinting a quarter of a mile in 58 seconds or less and then jogging the last three quarters. He held the image of himself running the first four-minute mile, so visualising his goal continuously. He also took up mountain-climbing, which helped him to develop his persistence and his ability to overcome any obstacles. Bannister ran his triumphant race on 6 May 1954, joining four of his quarter miles together to run the whole mile in 3 minutes 59.6 seconds.

What a brilliant example of creative goal-setting. When you break down your bigger objectives into smaller pieces, anything and everything becomes possible.

## Dream, fantasise, imagine!

Remember how your subconscious can work for you if it is filled with powerful positive images, beliefs and expectations. Let yourself relax and fantasise about whatever it is that you truly want, allowing your subconscious to work its creative best. Don't set any limitations at this stage. Never mind wondering if things are 'realistic' or 'possible'. Go way beyond your glass ceilings and let your imagination run riot. Daydreaming is like spreading your net over all that is possible; why not try it and see what dreams you can catch?

Einstein – a man who imagined riding on a beam of light in order to develop his theory of relativity – said that 'Imagination is more important than knowledge'. Mozart and Michelangelo both speak of the creative trances from which they gleaned their best ideas, and Steven Spielberg says he often gets inspiration when he is driving.

## TIME OUT

RELAX, CLOSE YOUR EYES AND THINK OF A TIME WHEN YOU FELT VERY ENTHUSIASTIC AND EXCITED BY SOMETHING. SEE THE SITUATION AND FEEL YOUR EMOTION. LET YOUR MEMORIES BE AS BRIGHTLY COLOURED AND VIVID AS YOU CAN MAKE THEM. REALLY GET INTO THE SKIN OF BEING THRILLED TO BITS. FEEL YOUR SPINE TINGLING WITH EXCITEMENT AND SENSE YOUR ENERGY BECOMING LIGHT AND FREE. SIT WITH THIS EXCITING FEELING FOR A WHILE.

WHEN YOU OPEN YOUR EYES, RECREATE THIS FEELING AGAIN. PRACTISE GENERATING EXCITEMENT AND YOU WILL BECOME VERY GOOD AT IT. PLEASURE IS SUCH A GREAT MOTIVATOR, SO LEARN HOW TO GET EXCITED ABOUT YOUR PLANS AND YOU WILL BE ALREADY MORE THAN HALFWAY TOWARDS REALISING YOUR GOALS.

# In your wildest dreams

Approach this exercise in a spirit of open-minded playfulness.
Take the eight areas of your life from your Life Wheel (see page
27). Now start to daydream about each one. Think big, think
creatively and think that anything is possible. Make your goals
really ambitious. And don't worry if your ideas seem to conflict.
Remember, anything goes. Write the results down in your
notebook. Below are a few examples to get you going. Your own
lists may be similar or totally different. Write what is meaningful
for you.

**Examples**
**Romantic relationships:** Find a terrific new, sensitive lover
who appreciates my sexuality. Go on a sexual gourmet course.
Live in Paris with a gorgeous new man. Meet my soul mate.
Have a fairytale white wedding. Fall in love.
**Personal growth:** Go on a retreat. Meditate regularly. Spend
a year in India. Live in an ashram. Study shamanism. Learn
Chinese.
**Friends and family:** Organise extravagant parties for my
friends. Get out much more! Stand up to my brother and stop him
bullying me. Take Mum on a world cruise.
**Money:** Double, no *treble*, my income by the end of the year.
**Happiness and creativity:** Start a belly-dancing class. Have
fun every day! Learn to throw pots. Be a sculptor. Exhibit my
work in central London. Open a restaurant.
**Confidence and self-image:** Become the most assertive
person I know. Lose a stone in the next six months. Start to love
myself. Go blonde! Look sexy. Be sexy.
**Health and wellbeing:** Run the London marathon. Become a
vegetarian. Learn to love my life and feel fabulous every day!
Have a baby. Move to the country. Lift weights.

**Career and life purpose:** Go freelance. Spend more time with my family. Write a bestselling novel. Be on television.

You should now have a list of interesting goals. It doesn't matter if they clash with each other (have a baby/run the marathon) or if some are less wildly ambitious than others. Look for your major life themes here. In other words, if you could give your goals a subject heading what might they be – for example 'Have an Adventure', 'Downsize and Slow Down', 'Explore my Sexuality', 'Develop a New Career'. What do your wildest dreams say about your current lifestyle? What clues do they give you about what you would like to change? Are you a closet extrovert who works in a small office every day and longs for the limelight? Would you really love to sell up and go travelling? Is your inner sex goddess longing to emerge? Would you love to make a living organising parties? Have you got a secret ambition? How will you feel in a year's time if you haven't done anything towards fulfilling any of your dreams?

We will look at this list again later; meanwhile just be aware that these creative ideas are drifting around in your head as you go about your day-to-day business.

---

We are often not even conscious of what we really want, deep down inside. Fifteen years ago I was standing at a bookstall at an alternative health conference. My favourite self-help book, by an author whom I greatly admired, was on sale. I picked up the book, turned to the person next to me and said, 'If you don't know which one to buy, I recommend this one.'

She replied, 'Why, did you write it?'

I said, 'No, but I wish I had.'

Five years later I had written my first self-help book and it was in the shops. I had forgotten this incident until only

# QUICK TIP

READING ABOUT GOAL-SETTING AND GOAL-GETTING IS GREAT, BUT IT IS ABSOLUTELY NO SUBSTITUTE FOR THE REAL THING. IN MY EXPERIENCE, THE GREATEST CONFIDENCE BOOSTER IS WHEN YOU ACTUALLY GET UP AND DO SOMETHING! ACTION IN PURSUIT OF GOALS IS THE BEST MOTIVATOR BY FAR.

SOME OF YOUR NEWLY IDENTIFIED GOALS WILL NEED LONG-TERM PLANNING BUT SOME WILL BE MORE SHORT-TERM. CHOOSE A SHORT-TERM GOAL (ACHIEVABLE IN THREE MONTHS OR LESS). IF YOU WERE TO BREAK THIS GOAL DOWN INTO SMALLER PIECES, WHAT WOULD THE FIRST STEP BE? TAKE THAT STEP NOW! MAKE THE PHONE CALL, PLAN THE MEETING, GO FOR A RUN, SIGN UP FOR THE COURSE, CLEAR OUT YOUR CLUTTER, SAY WHAT YOU HAVE TO SAY... WHATEVER STEP YOU NEED TO TAKE, TAKE IT NOW. AS SOON AS YOU BEGIN, YOU WILL FEEL LIKE A NEW PERSON AND THE NEXT STEP WILL BE EASY. TAKE ACTION EVERY DAY UNTIL THIS GOAL IS ACHIEVED. KEEP RESOLUTE AND KEEP GOING AND YOU CANNOT FAIL!

recently, when I realised that the seed of the idea to write a book had been planted on that day, three years before I consciously became inspired to start writing. When I think back to this incident now, I can vividly remember my feeling when the woman asked me if I had written the book. At first I was incredulous, but then I thought that, yes, if *she* considered it was possible, maybe it was. But, of course, what was much more important was the fact that *I* now felt that it was possible – and, as they say, the rest is history!

So don't discount your big dreams; they can come true if you really believe you can achieve them. Big dreams also contain the seeds of your real vision of who you are and what you want to be.

EXERCISE:

## Create a three-year vision

Fast-forward three years and look at your life. Imagine that you are reflecting on your progress.

- What has happened that pleases and delights you?
- How has your life changed for the better in the last three years?
- Describe your personal and working life in the present tense (as if these things have really happened).

Brainstorm for ideas and write down everything that comes to you. Try to be as detailed as you can. Make a strong and powerful image of your ideal life (what is happening and how you are feeling). Be ambitious; don't short-change yourself. Remember that *you will only make happen whatever you believe is possible for you.*

Now look through all your ideas and see how they fit into the categories of your Life Wheel. Do they suggest any steps that you might take towards any of your wildest dreams?

You will probably now be starting to get a clearer vision of the life you desire and some of the longer-term goals you really want to go for.

# Become a visionary

Visionaries are winners who create a positive future because they know how to make things happen. They do this by:

- **Identifying** their personal goals
- **Visualising** their goals and imagining just what it will be like to achieve them
- **Committing** themselves to reaching their goals within a certain time.
- **Acting as if** their goals have already materialised.

Follow these simple guidelines and see for yourself how effective they can be. You can create the life of your dreams – start now. Get focused.

---

## TIME OUT

### FIVE-MINUTE RELAXATION

THIS IS A WALKING MEDITATION, IN WHICH YOU FOCUS ON THE GENTLE WAY THAT YOUR FOOT MEETS THE GROUND AND RISES AGAIN. YOU CAN DO IT ANYWHERE – AS YOU WALK AROUND THE SUPERMARKET OR ON YOUR WAY TO WORK (IT'S A GREAT WAY TO BECOME CALM AND CENTRED EVEN IN THE RUSH HOUR!). IF YOU CAN WALK OUTSIDE, SO MUCH THE BETTER, BUT IT DOESN'T MATTER IF YOU JUST PACE AROUND INSIDE. AS YOU STEP FORWARDS, YOU ARE GROUNDING YOUR NEW IDEAS ABOUT HOW AND WHAT YOU WANT TO CHANGE IN YOUR LIFE; THAT IS, YOU ARE MAKING YOUR IDEAS REAL. KNOW THAT EVERY CONSCIOUS STEP YOU TAKE WILL BE A STEP TOWARDS MAKING THE CHANGES YOU NEED TO MAKE.

---

**1** TAKING THE FIRST STEP

IMAGINE THAT YOU ARE ABOUT TO TAKE THE FIRST STEP TOWARDS CHANGE. NOW, SYMBOLICALLY, TAKE THAT STEP.

**2** WALKING WITH AWARENESS

BRING YOUR TOTAL FOCUS TO EACH STEP THAT YOU TAKE. FEEL THE WAY THAT YOUR FOOT MEETS THE FLOOR, HOW IT COMPLETES A STEP AND THEN RISES AGAIN. BECOME TOTALLY AWARE OF THE WAY THAT YOU ARE WALKING. DON'T RUSH; JUST GO SLOWLY.

**3** LETTING THOUGHTS PASS BY

AS YOU ARE WALKING, LET ALL OTHER THOUGHTS PASS YOU BY. KEEP COMING BACK TO FOCUSING ON YOUR STEPS.

**4** FEELING THE REALITY OF THE EARTH

WHATEVER SURFACE YOU ARE WALKING ON, BECOME AWARE OF THE SOLIDITY OF THE EARTH BENEATH YOUR FEET. THE EARTH SUPPORTS YOUR EVERY MOVE, EVERY STEP OF THE WAY. LET THIS FEELING OF SOLIDITY REMIND YOU THAT THE UNIVERSE SUPPORTS YOU. ALLOW THIS KNOWLEDGE TO GIVE YOU THE CONFIDENCE TO MOVE FORWARD IN YOUR LIFE. WALK WITH AWARENESS FOR AS LONG AS YOU WISH.

# Step 3
# Keep Motivated

*Desire is the key to motivation,*
*but it's the determined commitment*
*to an unrelenting pursuit of your goal,*
*a commitment to excellence, that will*
*enable you to attain the success you*
*seek.*

MICHAEL JORDAN

Motivation is a driving force that makes you glad to jump out of bed in the morning, feeling full of yourself and happy to be alive. When you have it, life is magic, and when you don't have it, you need to get some quick! Don't make the mistake of thinking that the dynamic and motivated people you know are just lucky to be the way they are. Getting motivated and staying motivated are art forms, which should be taught in school but aren't, so we need to learn them.

Motivated people are passionate! They love what they do and they are full of themselves (in the nicest possible way). Their enthusiasm and excitement are catching and they attract other people's interest and attention. I've just been watching David Attenborough bringing the natural world to life on one of his fabulous programmes; now there's a motivated man.

**MOTIVATED PEOPLE**

In his seventies he is still creating awesome and original material that delights and fascinates huge audiences. By sharing his knowledge and passion he has spread important environmental and ecological messages to millions. David Attenborough is an example of a man with a mission who was always bound to succeed because he is a practical dreamer. Practical dreamers are in touch with their greatest passions and desires and they also know how to make their dreams reality.

I'm sure you know someone who is always talking about starting something new but never does it – or maybe they begin it but get sidetracked by early setbacks. We have all experienced that first flush of excitement at the prospect of a new goal, only to find that our energy and commitment just seem to run out too soon. This has certainly happened to me in the past. The times I haven't followed through have always been when my dream has felt unrealistic and I haven't created a workable plan of action. Think about a time when this has happened to you. What do you think stopped you achieving your goal?

It's very easy to get enthusiastic about a new idea, to get inspired by all the possibilities. And then we get down to the nuts and bolts and discover that there are very ordinary things to be done before we can see the realisation of our exciting initiative. This is where practical dreamers win through; they can maintain their vision even if the going gets rough. They are persistent and determined never to give up. When you next switch on the light, let yourself be inspired by Thomas Edison, who stood by his dream and gave us electric lighting after more than 10,000 failed attempts.

## Achieving your goals

People who achieve their goals do so with passion, planning, persistence and purpose.

### • Passion

Go back to your three-year vision and pick out the goals that you created in each of the categories of your Life Wheel. Some of these will be long term and others will be short term. Try to include one or two from each category of your wildest dreams list. Now rate your passion quotient for each goal on a scale of 1–10 (1 = slightly interested, 10 = passionate ). Do this quickly. Don't sit and think about it.

Any goal with a mark less than 10 won't stand a chance. Your commitment must be absolute or you will never be able to sustain the energy and drive to see your goal through. Now make a list of your top goals (the ones that scored 10).

## • Planning

Passion is the fuel that keeps you interested, and planning is the practical way forward. Practical dreamers change their visions into reality through careful planning.

First check that your goals are SMART – Specific, Measurable, Ambitious, Realistic and Timed. It's no good having a vague goal, such as 'be successful'. You must know exactly what you need to achieve in order to feel more successful. For example, if it means a career change, what specific steps will you have to take, how will you measure your progress and how long will it take? Keep your goals ambitious or you will never stretch beyond your old comfort zone. Be ready to reach for your best and set goals that are realistic for you (ones you believe you can achieve).

## • Persistence

Persistence is the quality of winners. Successful people never, ever give up. There may be obstacles, disappointment and challenges along the way (especially if you are going for some really big changes) and you must be ready to face them. Thomas Edison was reportedly asked, 'Why do you keep trying to create an electric light when you have already failed 10,000 times?' He is said to have answered, that he had not failed 10,000 times; rather, that he had successfully discovered 10,000 alternatives that didn't work, and with each of these discoveries he became closer to finding the one breakthrough that would succeed.

Persistence is not a matter of keeping on doing the same thing even if it doesn't work. No, persistence is hitting a brick wall and realising that you must find a way over it, around it, through it, under it or maybe even blow it up. Practical dreamers look for creative solutions to their setbacks and they keep on trying alternatives until they find one that works.

When the going gets rough, the tough just increase their self-belief and their determination to win through. Cultivate an image of yourself as a person who is a survivor who will always bounce back from any circumstance. Overcome the first hurdle and know that you are determined to succeed. Then go on to overcome the next hurdle. Celebrate every step along the way towards your goal and let each one serve to strengthen your resolve. Action makes you feel courageous. Keep moving forward and your self-belief will go through the roof. Remember that whenever you strive to reach your potential you are acting like a winner. You cannot fail, whatever happens!

## • Purpose

Imagine that you have achieved some of your goals and ask yourself what these accomplishments give you. Your answers will reveal your values, and these are what really drive you. For example, are you looking for ways to help others, create financial security, become more confident, contribute to life, feel better about yourself or spread happiness?

Your values demonstrate the essence of what really inspires you to reach for your dreams. Have a look at your list of goals and make a note of why you want to achieve them. Whenever you are working towards one of your key values you will be highly motivated to succeed. Think of the tireless work of such people as Mother Teresa, Mahatma Gandhi and Nelson Mandela, ordinary individuals whose dedication to a vision gave them superhuman power and resilience.

Of course, these are incredible examples of what can happen when dynamic values and strength of purpose are demonstrated in action. But don't think that your values have to be world-shatteringly impressive in order to work for you. They don't. For example, you might want to make more money so that you can feel a sense of security, or maybe you would love a promotion because it would increase your self-esteem. Always ask yourself why you want to achieve a goal and discover the deeper meaning and purpose behind your desire.

We are often inclined to link the idea of success with money and status but these things do not necessarily bring happiness. True success comes when we are living our lives to the full and loving and appreciating our moments. Act with integrity, know your values and your true purpose and don't forget to enjoy yourself as you take each step towards your goal.

**EXERCISE:**
_____

# Your future self

This exercise helps you to give added depth to your future visions by looking at your intuitive responses. Concentrate on your inner images and feelings rather than your thoughts – some of you will 'see' things and others will sense feelings; either way is fine. There is no need to force anything; just let pictures and emotions rise up spontaneously.

1 Close your eyes if you wish. Relax, slow your breathing and let go of any tension. Now fast forward to the future and *see* or *sense* yourself living the way you want to live. Take a good look at your future self. Do you look different? What is your body language like? What are your strongest feelings? What doubts have disappeared and what new strengths and abilities do you have?

2 Step into the shoes of your future self and ask yourself these questions:

   • Out of everything I have achieved, what has given me the greatest satisfaction?

   • What has made me happy?

   • What is the most important lesson I have learned?

   • How have I been able to help others?

   • What am I most proud of?

3 Discover exactly how you can achieve these successes by finishing the following sentences:

   • To reach these goals I need to be more…

   • I need to focus on…

   • I need to believe that I…

   • I need to be ready to…

   • I can start to achieve these goals now by…

---

Your intuition is a powerful sixth sense that you can always call upon to give clarity to a situation. Thinking can only tap into your beliefs, whereas your intuitive response bypasses thoughts and goes straight to the heart of the matter. Start to become aware of your immediate or 'gut' feelings – your intuition grows stronger the more that you use it.

---

## TIME OUT

STOP FOR A MOMENT AND LET GO OF ALL THOUGHTS ABOUT GOALS, ACHIEVEMENT AND SUCCESS. BELIEVE IT OR NOT, SELF-TRANSFORMATION CAN ONLY HAPPEN WHEN WE ARE ABLE TO ACCEPT OURSELVES TOTALLY (OUR WEAKNESSES AS WELL AS OUR STRENGTHS). SELF-ACCEPTANCE GIVES US THE GREEN LIGHT FOR CHANGE; IT GIVES US THE STRENGTH TO TAKE RISKS AND HELPS US TO LET GO OF ANY SELF-DOUBT THAT MAY STAND IN OUR WAY. TAKE SOME QUIET TIME NOW TO SIT AND BECOME AWARE THAT YOU REALLY ARE GOOD ENOUGH JUST THE WAY YOU ARE. YOU ARE COMPASSIONATE, LOVING AND KIND, AND YOU ARE ALWAYS DOING THE VERY BEST THAT YOU CAN. ACCEPT YOURSELF JUST AS YOU ARE IN THIS MOMENT ... AND THE NEXT, AND THE NEXT ...

---

## Coming through for yourself

If your vision of what you want and who you are does not fit with the reality of your life, you will feel dissatisfied and discontented. These feelings can send you either down into a cycle of negativity or up and onwards into a cycle of positivity. The choice is always yours.

When things are not so good it's easy to blame your circumstances, someone else or even yourself. I don't need to tell you that this approach will take you nowhere! Self-pity, self-doubt and self-criticism are like three wicked witches who will cast a spell of depression, despondency and inertia around you. You will have no buzz, no energy and no motivation. Whenever you feel stuck in this way just check your attitude and then change it! If you are sounding like Eeyore (gloomy and hopeless) try a bit of upbeat Tiggerish energy. Yes, 'the wonderful thing about Tiggers is Tiggers are wonderful things' (as the song goes); and the wonderful thing about you is that you are a wonderful thing!

Give yourself a break and view your problems as challenges that you can and will overcome. Think yourself up (I am great, I know I can do this) and never undervalue yourself to others. Imagine Tigger bouncing along; now see yourself with that same vibrant, optimistic energy. It feels good, doesn't it? When you radiate self-belief, you attract powerful positive energy from the universe: you suddenly find yourself in the right place at the right time; the person you most needed to see turns up out of the blue; new and exciting opportunities start to appear on your horizon.

The beautiful and talented Halle Berry, Bond girl and one of the most bankable stars in Hollywood, is the first black winner of a best actress Oscar in the 74-year history of the awards. In her acceptance speech Halle paid tribute to her mother: 'I want to thank my mom, who has given me the strength to fight every single day to be who I want to be and given me the courage to dream that this dream might be happening and is possible for me.' Halle knows that her mother's constant encouragement and support over the years have helped her to sustain the drive, focus and motivation that she has needed to create her amazing success story.

Raised by her mother, who had very little money, Halle was

bullied at school and called 'Zebra' and 'Half-breed' by other pupils. But it seems that these difficulties just made her try all the harder. Her best friend at school is not at all surprised that Halle has become an international celebrity. She says, 'No matter what Halle did, whether it was in school, homework, or in the playground, she gave 110 per cent. I guess she had more ambition and drive than anyone else.' Halle has had to work hard to get to the top of the Hollywood tree and it hasn't been easy for the African-American actress to find good roles. But even though the odds were stacked against her she knew that she could make it. And with continuous effort, dogged persistence and sheer grit she did!

Throughout her childhood Halle's mother was a hard-working, upbeat role model, who always showed complete faith in her daughter. Such positive parenting certainly helps to create the self-belief and determination that can lead to success in life, but it is not enough on its own. In the end the only person who can motivate you is yourself! If you feel that when you were a child your family was not always as support-ive as it might have been, just let that thought go; you can still come through for yourself.


## Get lucky

The writer James Joyce said to his biographer: 'Never under-estimate the element of luck. The first thing we want to know about someone is: are they lucky or unlucky? Do slates fall on their heads or do they win raffles?'

When I was at primary school there was a girl in my class who seemed to be able to do no wrong. She wasn't unusually brainy, beautiful or talented, but there was something about her that was bright and free and attractive, and everybody wanted some of it. She was Miss Popularity. All of us wanted to be her friend. Whenever anything great happened she was there in the thick of it, and she always got the most cards on Valentine's Day! Over the years, I have often thought about her and the magic that seemed to envelop her. Then, one day recently, I had an email from her (via the amazing Friends Reunited) and we met up. And after nearly 40 years, guess what? She is as blessed today as she was as a child.

The most interesting thing about her was her take on life. She told me that she had been 'so lucky' to meet her husband, get her great job, have her beautiful kids ... Her light-hearted and approachable manner were just the same as they had been at school. No wonder we all wanted to be her friend. We had a great afternoon and she was very good company. As we got to talk more about our lives she revealed that she had been divorced and brought up her children on her own for 10 years until she remarried. And, oh yes, she had suffered from breast cancer five years ago and felt so lucky that she was now fit and well. Even if a slate *had* fallen on her head, this woman would have found a great way to tell the tale!

I listened closely to the words she used. Her conversation was full of appreciation and enjoyment. She actually has had her fair share of what we might call 'bad luck', but, you know, she just didn't see it like that. I came away thinking that I'd like to meet up with her again. She confirmed my belief that if you believe you are lucky, then so you are.

This little piece of personal research fits nicely with the results of Dr Richard Wiseman's recent scientific study of why some people get to be luckier than others. He discovered that those who *think* they are lucky achieve more success and happiness because, without realising it, they are actually attracting good fortune into their lives. Dr Wiseman found that lucky people expect to be fortunate; they assume that their relationships will be happy and supportive, and that is exactly what they are.

Lucky people are good fun. They are generous with their time and attention and quick to recognise a good opportunity when it arises. If you radiate happy-go-lucky, light-hearted energy, you lift the spirits of others around you and before you know it they are responding in a more upbeat way. There is no doubt that lucky people see the positive potential in everything, and this is a fabulous gift that you can give to yourself.

# See the positive potential

Lucky people even use bad luck to their advantage; they see the positive potential in *everything* that happens to them. The following exercise shows you how you can do this yourself.

- Remember that things could be worse. Just think of those who are in a more terrible situation.

- Get things in perspective by looking at the bigger picture. However bad it looks, know that 'this too will pass'.

- Remember the lucky breaks that you have had in the past. Expect one now.

- Every cloud has a silver lining. Look for it.

- Learn from past mistakes and find new and creative ways to solve your problems.

- If bad luck strikes, don't assume that you are powerless. List your options and look for a solution.

---

Lucky people look on the bright side of life and make the most of all their experiences (the good as well as the bad). Open yourself to the charms of Lady Luck, expect the best and do all that you can to achieve it, and you will find new energy, excitement and motivation in everything you do. Try it today. You have everything to gain.

## Self-motivation

You are the only one who can make it happen for you. Others can support and encourage you, but you have to find the energy within in order to step into the centre of your own life and take charge. Many motivational psychologists believe that no one can ever be motivated to do something unless they actually *know for themselves* that they can do it, *and feel in their hearts that they want to*. In other words, you can only ever depend on yourself to give you the drive you need to keep going. Your self-motivation (or lack of it) will influence everything you do: your work, income, level of personal commitment, mood, relationships, determination and results. When you are working on improving your levels of self-motivation, you have to talk yourself into a positive emotional state. Any negative beliefs need only to be changed or redirected in order for you to feel your inner strength and resolve returning. With positive self-talk you can 'talk yourself up' and lift your mental, emotional and spiritual energies. This naturally leads to the kind of focused and effective action that accomplishes goals. In this way you can programme yourself to meet your challenges and also increase the belief that you can and will achieve whatever it is you are attempting to do. Try talking yourself up with the following positive, motivational statements.

- I am determined and motivated and nothing stops me.
- I feel great and am ready for anything.
- I love life and life loves me back.
- Today I am on top of the world; anything is possible.
- I go for my goals and I reach them; nothing stands in my way.
- I am not afraid of anyone or anything; I feel confident and assertive.
- Today I start my fabulous new life.
- I believe in myself 100 per cent and I am now ready to live my dreams.

- I never make excuses, I do things on time and I keep to my word.
- I am so lucky to be alive.

Repeat these statements out loud. Don't worry if you don't believe that they are true; the bigger the 'lie' you feel you are telling, the more powerfully the statement will be affecting your negative beliefs (we will look more closely at the way positive affirmations work in the next chapter). For now just notice how your energy changes when you make these upbeat declarations. Do they make you feel good? Say them again and again and again ... Keep motivated.

# TIME OUT

## FIVE-MINUTE RELAXATION

THE BEST THINGS IN LIFE ARE FREE! GO OUTSIDE AND NOTICE THE NATURAL WORLD. EVEN IF YOU ARE IN THE MIDDLE OF A CITY YOU CAN FIND A PARK, A TREE, A BIRD, SOME BLOSSOM. TAKE A FEW MINUTES AWAY FROM YOUR THOUGHTS TO APPRECIATE THE BEAUTY OF NATURE. LOOK AT THE PERFECTION OF A FLOWER, OF THE PASSING CLOUDS, THE SUNSHINE, THE RAIN. BE THANKFUL FOR THE BEAUTY THAT SURROUNDS YOU AND VALUE THE MIRACLE OF YOUR LIFE.

DON'T LET YOUR BUSYNESS TAKE YOU OVER COMPLETELY. FIND TIME EVERY DAY TO CONNECT WITH THE NATURAL RHYTHMS OF THE UNIVERSE. BECOME MORE AWARE OF THE NATURAL WORLD AND LOOK FOR THE WONDER THAT CONSTANTLY SURROUNDS YOU. IF YOU CAN DO THIS REGULARLY YOU WILL FEEL MORE GROUNDED AND IN TOUCH WITH YOUR EMOTIONS AND THOUGHTS. GIVE LOVE AND APPRECIATION TO LIFE AND YOU WILL FIND THAT IT WILL BE RETURNED TO YOU IN MANY WAYS.

TAKE A NATURAL BREAK WHENEVER YOU CAN AND REMIND YOURSELF THAT YOU ARE A CHILD OF THE UNIVERSE. FEEL YOUR DEEP CONNECTION WITH NATURE. YOU ARE A CREATURE OF THE EARTH AND THIS IS WHERE YOUR ROOTS LIE.

# Step 4
# Transform Negative Energy

*What is in you, let it out.*
*What you really want to do, do it.*
*Don't yield to doubt.*

In taking the first three steps to becoming your own life coach you are really setting yourself on the path to gaining control and activating brilliant new options for yourself. As you Reach for Your Best, Get Focused and Keep Motivated you will find yourself full of optimistic energy that will attract fresh and exciting opportunities. To maintain your momentum and enthusiasm you will need to stay in a positive state so that any obstacles or setbacks don't wreck your plans and throw you into indecision and self-doubt.

Many clients have told me that their greatest stumbling block is negative energy. And, yes, when you feel engulfed by waves of negativity who doesn't start to flag? Self-doubt can lead you to question your potential and your capacity to stay focused and highly motivated. The ability to transform negative into positive energy is vital for your success. Life's winners are not people who are always successfully achieving fabulous goals and live a glamorous life free of worry and concern. No, winners are ordinary people, just like you and me. They face the challenges that life brings to everyone, but they always come out of them stronger and more resilient. They have a fierce determination and they know how to fight back. And this is what makes all the difference between those who give up on their goals and those who go on to achieve them. It's not a question of personality or even ability; it all comes down to whether you know how to deal effectively with negative energy. If you are determined to achieve the success you desire, then you need to develop a positive approach to negativity. This is so easy to do; it just takes a simple change of attitude.

No one starts at the top. You have to make your way there, one positive believing step at a time. You may have seen the Oscar-winning film *Erin Brockovich*, which stars Julia Roberts in the title role. It tells the incredible story of one woman's campaign against big business and how she eventually won a quarter-billion-dollar settlement for a group of families who were seriously affected by water contamination. Erin Brockovich was a single parent who had a history of dead-end jobs and dead-end relationships; she was down but not out! She had to find great positive mental and emotional strength to fight her battle, and her eventual success was the result of a relentless quest to uncover the truth in the face of much negativity and opposition. The real Erin Brockovich really did transform a negative situation into something that was positive, and in the process she became confident and empowered. By channelling all her energies into the pursuit of her goal she became a folk heroine, and demonstrated the power of positive belief, purpose and action.

**POSITIVE PEOPLE**

## Take a positive approach to negativity

I have noticed that my clients often feel a real fear of becoming negative, and while they remain afraid they are unable to deal with their negativity. Now, I am going to let you in on an important secret: even highly positive people get the blues. It's hard to believe, I know, particularly on a day when your motivation is flagging. When you are feeling down, the rest of the world looks as though it has everything sussed. Everyone seems to be having brilliant relationships, doing fabulous jobs and feeling great, while you alone are struggling with your issues and feeling flat. But this is never true, of course; it just looks like this when you are feeling negative.

So let's stop being afraid of the N-word and try looking at it in a different way.

Being positive does not mean that you always have to look on the bright side of life and push anything negative under the carpet. Positive people look realistically at life and they are not afraid of their own or other people's negativity. So don't hide away from thoughts, feelings and behaviour that are unhelpful and unsupportive, but recognise negativity when it arises in yourself and others, and then deal with it so that it can work for you. This may mean, for example, making a decision not to spend time with someone who brings you down. A conscious choice not to be that person's victim would be a good way to convert a negative situation into a positive outcome.

A friend of mine was in a long-term relationship with a man when she began to think that he was seeing someone else. Naturally she felt devastated, her self-esteem plummeted and she lost all her bright energy and sparkle. But she is a survivor and she didn't stay in that dark place very long. She looked her own negativity in the eye (feelings of worthlessness and inadequacy) and began to rebuild her own sense of self-respect and value. When she felt strong enough she used her anger in a constructive way, transforming her negative energy into something powerful and assertive. She did this by directly challenging the man's behaviour. At first he responded with lame excuses and then he fell apart, admitting everything, and wept to be forgiven. By this time she had seen enough of him to realise that he wasn't worth taking back. In the end she said that she was glad to have gone through it all because the situation had uncovered his weaknesses and her own strengths.

This is a fine example of how to transform the negative and it demonstrates something of vital importance. If you look closely at any negative condition you will always see the possibility for change lying at its centre. Face up to negative energy, find out exactly how it affects your life and then you can take the necessary steps to overcome it, learn from it and move on. This is the positive approach to negativity, and it works every time. There are tools that you can use to overcome any form of negative energy and we will look at these shortly. Meanwhile just think back to an occasion when you faced your own self-doubt or the negativity of others and *moved on* out of this state. How did you do this? What personal qualities did you call upon? What did you learn about yourself?

# QUICK TIP

NAME THREE PERSONAL CHALLENGES THAT HAVE PUSHED YOU INTO A NEGATIVE STATE BUT WHICH YOU WENT ON TO OVERCOME. LOOK AT EACH ONE SEPARATELY AND ASK YOURSELF THE FOLLOWING QUESTIONS. WHY DID I GO UNDER? HOW LONG DID I STAY THERE? WHAT CHANGE IN ATTITUDE CAUSED MY ENERGY TO LIFT AND ENABLED ME TO FACE MY CHALLENGE? HOW DID I OVERCOME MY NEGATIVITY? HOW DO I FEEL NOW THAT I LOOK BACK AT THIS SITUATION?

LOOKING BACK AT DIFFICULTIES IS A VERY POSITIVE ACT. THROUGH DOING IT YOU WILL DISCOVER MUCH ABOUT YOURSELF, YOUR RESOURCEFULNESS, YOUR INNER STRENGTH AND YOUR CAPACITY TO BOUNCE BACK. USE THIS AWARENESS TO REMIND YOU THAT YOU CAN AND WILL OVERCOME ANYTHING THAT PRESENTS ITSELF TO YOU IN THE FUTURE.

# Get into the positive flow

You bring your whole self – your thoughts, feelings and behaviour – to each experience. When you are feeling positive and confident, your energy is light, freely flowing and uncluttered; your thoughts are optimistic; you feel secure and centred, and your actions are assertive and assured. Imagine that your personal energy circuit is in this relaxed and free-flowing mode right now. This is your natural state of balance. It allows you to reach your creative best in all that you do. When you feel like this absolutely nothing can stand in your way! Remember a time when you felt like this. Wasn't it fantastic?

Actually we are the ones who stop our own creative flow, by allowing negative energy to block our energy circuit and disrupt our positive state. A self-critical thought creates a chain reaction, which will affect us at all levels. For example the thought 'I'm not good enough' plunges us into a negative state of pessimism and depression, which then leads straight to indecision and inaction. No need to remind yourself of how terrible this can feel!

The great news is that once you know how your personal energy circuit works, you can easily find and transform your negative blocks and so create that balanced and positive feeling of wellbeing. Changing your energy will change your life. The checklist below shows some examples of the way that negative energy can affect us at all levels. Notice how every negative characteristic has within it the possibility of being transformed into a positive one.

# Energy checklist

| NEGATIVE ENERGY | POSITIVE ENERGY |
|:---:|:---:|
| TRANSFORMS TO → | |

| Negative thoughts | Positive thoughts |
|:---:|:---:|
| I don't believe in myself | I believe in myself |
| I am not deserving | I deserve the best |
| I am a victim | I am in control |
| I am powerless | I am powerful |
| I am a failure | I am a success |
| I can't change | I can change |

| Negative emotions | Positive emotions |
|:---:|:---:|
| I feel insecure | I feel secure |
| I feel trapped | I feel free |
| I feel dull | I feel enthusiastic |
| I feel stuck | I feel motivated |
| I feel lethargic | I feel energetic |
| I feel guilty | I feel clear |

| Negative behaviour | Positive behaviour |
|:---:|:---:|
| I can't take risks | I can take risks |
| I can't say no | I can say no |
| I can't show my feelings | I can show my feelings |
| I act indecisively | I act decisively |
| I act passively/aggressively | I act assertively |
| I have poor communication skills | I have good communication skills |

# Thinking positively

Who wants to struggle through life believing that they are powerless when they can just as easily recognise their true power and become the best they can be? Who wants to think that they are a failure when instead they could be enjoying success? You certainly don't want to limit yourself in this way, do you?

And you don't have to, your negative thoughts and beliefs have no power over you; you can change them as soon as you recognise them. Take a look at the negative thoughts in the previous list. Perhaps there are one or two that you particularly relate to. Are there any of your own that spring to mind? Think about this for a while and then make a list of your most common negative thoughts. Every time you repeat a thought, you reaffirm its significance. You don't even have to speak it; the thought is enough. Why keep on repeating something that only limits and restricts you? At least 70 per cent of our daily thoughts are negative (and what percentage on a bad day?). Any reduction in this figure will make a huge impact on your life, taking you into that elite band of winners who know and experience the true power of positivity.

By making positive affirmations instead of negative ones you can create a new cycle that is powered by positive energy. Try running through the list of positive thoughts from the checklist. Say them out loud to yourself. Look in the mirror and repeat them again. Create your own positive thoughts that have special meaning to you and then say them over and over again. The more often you do this the more powerful the result will be, as you alter the way you think by replacing your old negative thought patterns with powerful upbeat energy. Notice how your spirit lifts as you think positively and how it falls when you think negatively. Always use your thoughts to inspire and energise yourself. Think positive and you will feel amazing.

---

# TIME OUT

RELAX AND TAKE A REST FOR A FEW MINUTES. TAKE SOME DEEP BREATHS AND CLOSE YOUR EYES.

THINK OF YOUR LIFE AS A JOURNEY AND A QUEST. WHERE ARE YOU GOING AND WHAT ARE YOU LOOKING FOR? WHAT STAGE ARE YOU AT IN YOUR JOURNEY? LET ANY IMAGES AND THOUGHTS ARISE NATURALLY.

ARE YOU EXPERIENCING ANY OBSTACLES ON THE PATH YOU HAVE TAKEN? DO YOU FEEL THAT YOU ARE OPEN TO ALL THE POSITIVE ENERGY THAT IS AVAILABLE TO YOU? AGAIN, GIVE YOURSELF TIME TO SENSE YOUR TRUE FEELINGS.

RECOGNISE THAT THIS IS YOUR PATH AND YOURS ALONE. VISUALISE YOUR UNIQUE JOURNEY TAKING YOU ALONG A LOVING AND POSITIVE PATH. IMAGINE ALL THE WONDERFUL EVENTS AND FASCINATING PEOPLE THAT WAIT FOR YOU. OPEN YOURSELF TO THE POSITIVE ENERGY OF THE UNIVERSE AND STEP ALONG YOUR SHINING PATH WITH EASE AND GRACE.

WHEN YOU ARE READY, OPEN YOUR EYES AND COME BACK TO YOURSELF. YOU ARE UNIQUE AND SPECIAL AND SO IS YOUR JOURNEY.

---

# Feeling positive

Nobody enjoys handling their negative emotions. None of us wants to feel miserable, sad or depressed. And feelings like anger, jealousy and shame are almost unmentionable. Have you ever rejected a feeling because you thought it was negative? Have you ever felt down, for example, and then hidden it because you wanted to put on a happy 'positive' face? It's fine to do this as long as you are conscious of what you are doing and are aware of how you are really feeling. In life coaching we often use the phrase 'fake it until you make it', and this is a good tactic as it helps you to tap into your assertive positive energy. But our negative (feel-bad) emotions need to be looked at and recognised before we can let go of them, or they just hang around and pop up again at some inappropriate time. So fake it by all means, but don't forget to look your real feelings in the face when the time is right: positive people are in touch with their feelings. Don't be afraid of your feelings; they can't hurt you and they have no power over you unless you deny them.

Take guilt. If you feel guilty take a closer look and discover what this feeling is telling you. Dig deeper and find what lies behind it. Why do you feel guilty? Is the feeling real or are you just being a victim? Can you do anything to redeem the situation? If so, do it and then move on. And if there's nothing you can do, then it's time to let go.

Take anger. Why are you angry? Is there a deeper reason behind this? Who are you angry with? Does something need to be said? Does something need to be done? Do you need to forgive yourself, or someone else?

Feelings are related to needs and if your needs are being met, then you can be optimistic and upbeat. If you are denying or hiding your feelings, you are pretending that you have no needs and you will feel full of negative energy. Positive people transform negative emotions by facing their feelings and dealing with them.

Take any of your negative emotions and find out what really lies behind them. Take whatever action feels appropriate and then let go! Just drop it. You are free to move on and feel positive.

Get into the habit of giving yourself *feeling checks* through-out the day. Whenever you remember, stop for a moment and ask yourself, 'What am I feeling right now?' As you get used to doing this you will become more in touch with your own feelings. You will find it easier to deal with difficult emotions and will be able to transform any negative emotional energy before it takes hold. Keep listening to your feelings, because they are trying to tell you something.

## Take positive action

If you want to walk on water you have to get out of the boat! I know, you weren't planning on miracles, you only want to change your life. But the principle is the same: if you keep doing what you have always been doing, you will get what you have always been getting. We all have our own personal behaviour patterns which can hold us back and restrict our action. If you want to make new things happen, you must be ready to change the way you behave. This means being able to ask for what you want and then being prepared to follow through with assertive action. You may not have to get out of the boat but you will certainly have to be ready to rock it! Are you ready to take this risk? Yes, it can feel like a risk (let's face it, if it wasn't such a challenge you would have done it before wouldn't you?).

# QUICK TIP

IMAGINE THAT YOU ARE ABOUT TO OPEN THE DOOR TO A ROOM WHERE A PARTY IS GOING ON. YOU STEP INSIDE AND LOOK AROUND, AND WHAT DO YOU NOTICE? WELL, YOU SEE THE PEOPLE AND THE ROOM, BUT THIS IS NOT ALL THAT YOU TAKE IN. AT A SUBTLER LEVEL YOU ARE *SENSING* THE ENERGIES OF EVERYONE THERE. YOU CAN FEEL THE ENERGETIC VIBRATIONS IN THE ROOM. IF THERE IS A BUZZ IN THE AIR YOU MAY 'CATCH' THE EXCITEMENT, AND IF THE ENERGY IS LOW YOU WILL PROBABLY GET A SINKING FEELING IN YOUR SOLAR PLEXUS AND START LOOKING FOR THE NEAREST EXIT. OTHER PEOPLE'S ENERGY CAN HAVE A DIRECT EFFECT ON THE WAY WE FEEL, AND YOU DON'T NEED TO HAVE CLAIRVOYANT POWERS TO SENSE AT THIS INTUITIVE LEVEL. WE ARE ALL PICKING UP ON THE THOUGHTS AND FEELINGS OF OTHERS AS WE GO ABOUT OUR DAILY BUSINESS, BUT WE ARE OFTEN DOING THIS UNCON-SCIOUSLY.

THINK ABOUT THAT TIME WHEN YOU WERE FEELING GREAT AND YOU MET SOMEONE WHO WAS FULL OF COM-PLAINTS AND MOANS. WHAT HAPPENED TO YOUR BRILLIANT MOOD? UNLESS YOU ARE CONSCIOUSLY AWARE OF THE ENERGY THAT SURROUNDS YOU, IT'S POSSIBLE TO BE DRAGGED DOWN INTO THE PITS OF NEGATIVITY WITHOUT EVEN REALISING HOW IT HAPPENED. START TO TUNE INTO OTHERS AND FEEL THE ENERGY THAT THEY ARE RADIATING. IF YOU SPEND TIME WITH POSITIVE AND UPBEAT PEOPLE YOU WILL 'CATCH' THEIR ENERGY.

Think now about any positive action you could take that would make a significant change to your life. It doesn't have to be something huge, let it be a small step that you know you can take. Why haven't you done this already? What have you been waiting for? Are you afraid that you might fail or that someone might not like you any more? Whose life are you living? Positive action makes you feel courageous. Decide to take an assertive step into your new life. You can do it!

Look around you at the moaners and whingers who sound and act just like victims. I'm not talking about people who have a genuine problem but about those who are always blaming something or someone for their troubles. Such 'victims' never have to bear responsibility for anything, or risk 'failing' or making a fool of themselves or stepping out of line. And there they stay, at the bottom of the pile, unhappy, resentful, full of regrets and low in self-esteem. I'm sure you know people like this. Notice how deeply unhappy and unfulfilled they are; with all their energy used up in complaining they never have the positive strength to move forward and create changes. But who wants to get to the end of their wonderful life having proved that they were only victims all along? Life is too precious and too short to sit around regretting lost opportunities.

You are different. You are a positive person and you take responsibility for creating the life of your dreams. So raise your expectations, step out of your comfort zone, smash through your glass ceilings. You are ready to act assertively.

# 10 tips for assertiveness

1 Be decisive.

2 Say no when you need to.

3 Take responsibility for your own actions.

4 Use good, clear communication skills.

5 Be an attentive listener.

6 Say yes when you need to.

7 Bring out the best in others and yourself.

8 Ask for what you want.

9 Don't be afraid to take a chance.

10 Stand up for yourself.

**EXERCISE:**

# Reviewing your behaviour

• Think of a time when you let a situation or a person victimise you.

How did you act?

What was the outcome?

What positive (assertive) action could you have taken to change the outcome?

• Now think of a time when you behaved assertively.

How did you act?

What was the outcome?

Look at your answers above and find at least one tip that would be useful for you to start using immediately. Use it!

# Keep things in perspective

The most obvious characteristic of a positive person is their ability to laugh at life and keep things in perspective. Sometimes it's possible for us to get so serious about living that we forget what it's really all about. It's easy to get wound up in this way when there are so many things to achieve and *so little time to get them all done*. But wait, let's stop a moment and reconsider this. When everything feels like such a big deal we can find ourselves lurching from one drama to another, locked into our negative responses. Think about your latest 'drama' and how it affected your thoughts, feelings and behaviour. When we react to situations and people in a fire-fighting manner we lose our perspective and often make our problems even harder to resolve.

So why not loosen up (the sky won't fall in) and try another way. Don't be afraid that you will lose control as soon as you take a more relaxed approach; this isn't true. Your lasting successes depend upon more than just reaching a particular goal; they also depend on your feel-good factor. By all means get focused, determined and motivated, but remember to *enjoy* your experiences. The greatest achievers also bring their positive energy to their relationships, and people love this! We all want some of that relaxed and fun-filled light-hearted energy and we will go out of our way to get some. In other words, when you can bring humour and perspective to any situation, you are much more likely to achieve all the help you need along the way.

Radiate positivity and you will attract positive energy into your life (supportive people, great opportunities and fun!). The next time you find yourself taking things too seriously for your own good, think to yourself, 'How important will this be in six months time?' Lighten up, smile, expect the best, act assertively and things will just start to come together. Transform negative energy.

---

# TIME OUT

## FIVE-MINUTE RELAXATION

GET COMFORTABLE, RELAX YOUR BODY AND RELAX YOUR MIND. CLOSE YOUR EYES AND FOLLOW YOUR BREATHING, IN AND OUT, IN AND OUT, IN AND OUT ... AND SOON YOU WILL FIND THAT YOUR BUSYNESS HAS SLOWED DOWN AND THAT YOU ARE MUCH CALMER AND MORE ALERT.

NOW IMAGINE THAT LOVE AND KINDNESS ARE POURING INTO YOUR HEART. FEEL HOW MUCH YOU ARE LOVED AND APPRECIATED. MAKE THIS FEELING EVEN STRONGER AND BIGGER UNTIL YOUR HEART IS OVER-FLOWING WITH LOVE AND KINDNESS. STAY WITH THIS FEELING FOR A WHILE.

YOU ARE SO FULL OF LOVE AND POSITIVE ENERGY THAT YOU WANT TO SEND IT OUT INTO THE WORLD. START BY SENDING THIS ENERGY TO YOUR LOVED ONES. IN YOUR MIND'S EYE SEE THEM LOOKING POSITIVE AND STRONG AND HAPPY. IS THERE ANYONE ELSE YOU CAN THINK OF WHO COULD DO WITH SOME OF THIS POWERFUL ENERGY? SEND THEM SOME.

---

NOTICE THAT THE MORE YOU RADIATE THIS LOVING ENERGY, THE MORE FABULOUS YOU FEEL.

NOW, SLOWLY, OPEN YOUR EYES, MAINTAINING THIS WARM LOVING FEELING. YOU TAKE YOUR LOVING ENERGY WHEREVER YOU GO. JUST TAP INTO IT WHEREVER YOU ARE: AT WORK, ON A TRAIN, PICKING UP THE KIDS FROM SCHOOL, COOKING, OUT TO DINNER ... PRACTISE RADIATING POSITIVITY AND YOU WILL FEEL AND LOOK FABULOUS. AND JUST SEE HOW WONDERFULLY OTHERS REACT!

# Step 5
# Be Inspired

*Basically, you wish yourself well ...*
*Desire by itself is not wrong. It is the*
*choices you make that are wrong. To*
*imagine that some little thing – food,*
*sex, power, fame – will make you happy*
*is to deceive oneself. Only something as*
*vast and deep as your real self can make*
*you truly and lastingly happy.*

SRI NISARGADATTA MAHARAJ

Life is like a box of chocolates, glamorously packaged and temptingly displayed. Each centre is irresistibly delicious but short-lived. If we compulsively eat our way through the box, each succeeding chocolate tastes less and less scrumptious and we end up feeling sick. This is how it is with life's material goodies; they deliver a quick buzz and then we are off looking for another thrill. Now don't think I'm belittling life's pleasures. I love them as much as the next person; I just know that they can never give the fulfilment and satisfaction that I crave. They are not enough. And we all know this deep down. We have probably all thought, 'There has to be more to life than this.' Glitzy 21st-century advertising makes such extravagant claims:

just use this toothpaste and you will become totally confident; wear that lipstick and every man in the room will want your phone number; wash your hair with this shampoo and you will look like a film star; go on that diet and you will have the figure of a model ... Promises, promises! Of course we want to look good and feel great; we want gorgeous shoes and a nice car *and* we want to feel a sense of true meaning and purpose in our life. The good news is, we can have all these things when we know how to balance the material and spiritual parts of our lives.

Don't be put off by the word spiritual. It doesn't mean that you have to restrict your diet, live in a cave in the Himalayas, or contemplate the meaning of life for hours. Although many traditional spiritual paths encouraged people to withdraw from the 'distractions' offered by the material world, much modern spirituality recognises that we may not have the time or the inclination to go on special retreats or undergo lengthy meditation practices. The challenge for us in the 21st century is to learn to harmonise our spiritual awareness with our material desires.

Sometimes we may be inclined to see our material and spiritual aspects as being separate or even in conflict with each other. But of course we need both. Our material form would not be alive without our spirit (life force), and obviously our spirit would be unable to exist in the physical world without a body. We all operate at physical, emotional and spiritual levels, and this is why we can never be *totally* fulfilled by anything that the material world has to offer. Money and the things it buys can never satisfy our deeper emotional and spiritual needs.

# Material and spiritual considerations

What do you consider to be the six most valuable things in your life? These can be items that you possess, people who share your life, gifts or abilities that you have ... They can be whatever you like.

Describe why each of them is so important to you.

The genie of the lamp has now appeared and offered you three wishes. What do you wish for? Explain your choices.

Imagine that you are at a party to celebrate your very long life. In your extreme old age what would you like to have achieved? What do you think would mean most to you at this time of your life?

Consider your answers. What do they reveal to you? How important are material considerations? How important is a deeper sense of fulfilment and purpose? How can you balance the material with the spiritual?

What are your true valuables? Appreciate them and cherish them every day.

## You are divine

Yes, you really are! You are human and so by definition you are spiritual; your spiritual self expresses itself through your material form. Universal energy flows through you and gives you life – that divine spark of consciousness that we all share. Think of the way that a light bulb depends on the electricity supply; you depend upon the universal energy source in exactly the same way.

Although your spirituality is a fundamental part of your being, you may still be wondering exactly what it is. After all, what is there to see? Rather than looking for external proof we need only to look inside ourselves to feel the inspiration and joy that our spiritual nature brings, and I'll explain how to do this in this chapter. If you have ever seen a newborn baby you will know, without a doubt, that we enter the world enfolded and embraced in glorious spiritual energy; we really do come trailing clouds of glory. Babies emanate their spirituality. You can *feel* the divine spark within them. And you, of course, were once like this too. In all likelihood, as your material pre-occupations began to fill your life, you started to forget your divinity. You got so busy doing that you lost touch with your being. Developing your spiritual awareness does not require extensive training and esoteric methods; you only need to reconnect with an experience that you have known all along but have forgotten about.

## Spiritual energy

Your spirituality gives you your love of life and so offers the ultimate gift. When you are feeling inspired you are actually connecting with your spiritual energy. Have you ever felt a sense of oneness with the rest of the universe? Perhaps you were watching a beautiful sunset or had fallen madly in love or had even just got carried away by something and lost all track of time.

Whenever your mind becomes totally concentrated and absorbed, you begin to experience a sense of unity with something much greater than yourself. Time stands still and you feel a shift in your awareness beyond your physical senses. Any activity that stills and calms your mind, such as yoga, visualisation or aerobic exercise, will trigger this shift, as will anything that unexpectedly affects you at a deep level, such as a dream

# QUICK TIP

START TO NOTICE THE LEVELS OF YOUR BUSYNESS. FOCUSED ACTION ACHIEVES OUTCOMES, BUT IT IS ALSO POSSIBLE TO GET INTO BEING BUSY JUST FOR ITS OWN SAKE. IF YOU DO TOO MUCH OF ANYTHING, YOU WILL FEEL STRESSED. THIS INCLUDES ALL FORMS OF BUSYNESS, INCLUDING TOO MUCH THINKING!

WHEN YOU START OVER-REVVING (YOU KNOW WHAT THIS FEELS LIKE), STOP IMMEDIATELY, WHATEVER YOU ARE DOING. REMIND YOURSELF THAT ALTHOUGH RUSHING AROUND MAY SEEM LIKE THE ONLY WAY TO GET EVERYTHING DONE, THIS IS NOT SO. YOU ARE AT YOUR MOST PRODUCTIVE WHEN YOU ARE CALMLY FOCUSED, AND THIS MEANS BEING ABLE TO SAVOUR EACH MOMENT FOR ITS OWN SAKE. SURE, THERE'S A JOB TO BE DONE, BUT UNLESS YOU CAN FIND THE PLEASURE AND MEANING IN YOUR TASK, THEN WHAT IS THE POINT?

- THE NEXT TIME YOU ARE FEELING FRAZZLED, JUST LET YOURSELF BECOME CONSCIOUS OF WHAT'S HAPPENING.

- REMEMBER THAT YOU ARE CHOOSING TO GET LOST IN BEING BUSY.

- TAKE A FEW SECONDS JUST TO STAND AND STARE AND BECOME AWARE OF YOUR BEINGNESS AS OPPOSED TO YOUR DOINGNESS.

- RETURN TO YOUR TASK IN THIS MORE RELAXED STATE AND YOU WILL FIND THAT WHATEVER YOU ARE DOING WILL BECOME EASIER AND YOU WILL FEEL CLEARER AND CALMER.

or a memory or an extreme emotion. To feel such a change in awareness you need only to be open-minded and open-hearted. Whenever your defences are down you will be able to feel your spiritual connection very powerfully.

Can you remember the last time you had a vivid experience like this? Next time you feel such a change in your energy recognise it for what it is and consciously go with it. Whenever you can tap into your spiritual energy you become inspired to reach for the very best within you. This connection helps you to understand the true significance and purpose of your life; it gives you a glimpse of the bigger picture and reminds you of who you really are – a fabulous divine being who is learning how to be human! When you feel inspired you attract the most powerful energy in the universe. You are going with the flow and everything starts to come together in an almost miraculous way.

## Beyond motivation and into inspiration

Highly motivated people always have the edge because they are super-charged with positivity, dynamic, focused, flexible, persistent and practical enough to be able to bring their vision into reality. But they have something extra too, and it's linked to a magical exuberance that is powerfully charismatic.

Several years ago, my husband and I moved to a small fishing village in Cornwall, where we encountered Tim Smit and his family. Tim had just arrived from London. He was in the music business and had built a recording studio in his house; however, he was really inspired by the natural beauty of Cornwall and soon began to uncover the mysterious Lost Gardens of Heligan. But even as we watched his amazing plan unfolding and the beautiful Heligan Gardens opening to huge public acclaim, Tim was already working on his next inspired idea. As he worked at Heligan, he had become increasingly fascinated by the world of plants and their importance to the survival of our species and to the planet. His broader canvas became the Eden Project, the so-called Eighth Wonder of the World.

I can vouch for the fact that Tim is a real man of the people, down to earth and a great participator in village life. There's nothing remotely airy-fairy or mystical about him. But his ideas are touched by the magic of inspiration and so they uplift and motivate all the people who work with him and around him. I'm sure Tim would agree that in a spiritual sense he was undoubtedly *led* to Cornwall to fulfil his fantastic mission.

If motivation is the icing on the cake, I think inspiration can be described as the cherry. Whenever a person feels inspired they carry an *extra* sense of purpose and clarity: they are spiritually connected and 'in the flow' and feel that they are being guided along their true path.

**EXERCISE:**

# Going with the flow

When you are going with the flow, you feel that you are in the right place at the right time, doing what you are supposed to be doing. Think of a time when you felt like this. Perhaps you were in a great relationship or you had started a new and exciting project.

Close your eyes and remember how you felt at the time – your excitement and enthusiasm, your motivation, your sense of 'can do'. Get right into the skin of those upbeat and inspiring emotions. Feel yourself reaching and achieving your best. Now, with your eyes still closed, 'see' yourself in this positive mode. Notice how you looked, your body language, your smile! Get right into the part again and recreate your go-getting mode.

Make your visualisation as three-dimensional as you can – the bigger and more vivid it is, the more powerful will be its effect.

Repeat this exercise whenever you need to be reminded of how good life can be for you. The more you can imagine yourself in the flow, the easier it becomes to draw this reality into your life. Your energy attracts your circumstances, so get into the positive and inspirational flow of your own energy and the rest will just fall into place. Keep practising this exercise.

---

## Get inspired

The quotation at the beginning of this chapter says that 'only something as vast and deep as your real self can make you truly and lastingly happy'. I'm glad to be able to tell you that this real self is close by and easy to access; all you have to do is tap into your spiritual awareness and get inspired!

We are such busy bees, and of course we need to be to keep all our shows on the road. But (as I am constantly saying), we are not called human *doings* – we are called human *beings*. Consider this for a moment. Now, think of *doing* as describing your activity out in the world and think of *being* as describing your inner (spiritual) awareness. You are in touch with your real self when your being and doing are in balance. The big question is: how much doing are you doing and how much being are you being?

The movers and the shakers of this world know that their time outs are an integral part of their ability to be productive. Remember how Einstein came to understand relativity by imagining riding a beam of light? Time outs are moments when you step out of doing mode into being mode, and they are vital if you are going to be creative, happy and successful in your life. As you reach for your best and go for your goals, don't forget to tap into your spiritual awareness. Let yourself become inspired to bring your visions into reality.

Look around at the people you admire most. You will find that they probably have a wide range of skills, talents and qualities. They are not one-dimensional people; they call on everything they've got to make their lives rich and meaningful. This inevitably means that they recognise the importance of balancing their spiritual awareness with their material consid-erations. It's interesting that many of our A-list celebrities have developed a long-standing interest in matters spiritual; for example Richard Gere (a practising Buddhist for many years), Madonna and Geri Halliwell (both practitioners of Ashtanga Yoga) and Sting (whose interest in Tantric Yoga has been well publicised) all speak of the important balancing role that their spiritual development has in their lives.

Why not emulate positive and effective role models – those who demonstrate that they are not just 'can do' people but also 'can be' people. Let the mantra *can do, can be* become part of your daily life.

## The importance of personal fulfilment

Anthony Robbins, a great motivational writer and speaker, has made this interesting observation: 'Goals are a means to an end, not the ultimate purpose of our lives. They are simply a tool to concentrate our focus and move us in a direction. The only reason we really pursue goals is to cause ourselves to expand and grow. Achieving goals by themselves will never make us happy in the long term; it's who you become, as you overcome the obstacles necessary to achieve your goals, that can give you the deepest and most long-lasting sense of fulfilment.'

# TIME OUT

THIS SEEMS LIKE AN APPROPRIATE MOMENT TO TAKE A TIME OUT!

RELAX, CLOSE YOUR EYES AND ALLOW YOUR BREATHING TO SLOW DOWN. CHOOSE A QUALITY THAT YOU WOULD LIKE TO EXPERIENCE MORE OF, SUCH AS LOVE, SPIRITUAL AWARENESS, CREATIVITY, FORGIVENESS ... OR ANYTHING ELSE YOU WISH. IMAGINE THAT YOUR QUALITY HAS A BEAUTIFUL COLOUR. NOW SEE YOURSELF BEING FILLED WITH THIS COLOUR AND FEEL THE POWER OF THIS QUALITY CIRCULATING THROUGH YOUR BODY, MIND AND SPIRIT. SEE AND FEEL THIS ENERGY WITHIN YOU. REMAIN WITH THIS FOR AS LONG AS YOU LIKE. AS YOU COME BACK TO THE ROOM AND OPEN YOUR EYES, LET THIS QUALITY STAY WITH YOU.

In pursuit of your dreams you learn to face your tests and bounce back from setbacks, and each time you do this you become more resilient, self-reliant and confident. There will always be complications and difficulties to overcome as you move onwards and upwards. Accept this and deal with it. If things were always easy, you would never need to stretch yourself that little bit further and you would never discover how tough, flexible and creative you can be. *Who you can become* will always hold more fascination for you than any goal that you might achieve.

# Amanda's story

Amanda was always an academic high-flyer, with straight As and a first-class degree. By the time she finished university and started to work as a journalist on a provincial paper she had become a can do, *must do* person. In other words, she had become a compulsive goal-getter. She came to see me because she was about to make a move to London to become a features writer for a famous glossy fashion magazine. This was the final step in a long-term plan that she had made when she was about 14. The next 10 years had flown by in a whirlwind of achievements and academic success, and here she was about to take the job of her dreams, so why was she feeling so utterly miserable?

The job was a fabulous one and she couldn't understand her sudden lack of energy and enthusiasm. The fact was, however, that now she had got what she had been working towards for all those years, the chase was over (or that was how it felt). Because she had been so focused on her career, Amanda had very little social life. She had lived at home with her parents while she worked on the local paper, and now all that was about to change.

Amanda realised that she had become a compulsive achiever and that it was time to relax and celebrate her great success, but this was hard to do. She felt organised and in charge of her life when she was following a structured plan and was afraid to let go of that control and relax into her life, although she knew she needed to do this. She decided to concentrate on increasing her 'being' activities and got involved in yoga and meditation. Six months after her move to London, Amanda had become a much happier person, less serious, more light-hearted and with an active social life. She said that she felt more rounded and complete and that her life had finally taken off.

If you have lost your inspiration in life, you may need to balance your activities with some more inward-looking pursuits. It will make all the difference to how you feel inside.

## 30 Easy ways to feel inspired

1 Take regular time outs. Make frequent stops throughout the day, even if only for a few seconds.
2 Look for the beauty that surrounds you, wherever you are.
3 Appreciate someone and tell them how you feel.
4 Do some activity that will calm your mind – take a sauna, practise yoga or t'ai chi, go for a swim ...
5 Follow your inspirational ideas.
6 Stand barefoot on the beach and inhale the ozone.
7 Start a conversation with a stranger.
8 Forgive someone.
9 Become absorbed in doing something you love.
10 Buy some flowers for your desk at work.
11 Make a collage of your favourite photos.
12 Treat yourself to a new novel and curl up and read it ... bliss!
13 Take the longer view and reflect upon who you are becoming rather than what you are doing.
14 Perform an act of kindness (and keep it to yourself).
15 Make something (anything) and get those creative juices flowing.
16 Become aware of your hunches and gut feelings – are they trying to tell you something?
17 Listen to your favourite music (and do nothing else).
18 When in doubt ask yourself what your heart feels.
19 Give something to someone.

**20** Spend time having fun with a small child.

**21** Write a letter to someone you love.

**22** Pretend this is your last day on earth – make the most of it.

**23** Go for a walk.

**24** Remember that you are divine.

**25** Dance around the house to loud music with a great beat.

**26** Take a trip to the countryside or a park.

**27** Do something you have never done before.

**28** Smile and enjoy your day.

**29** Imagine that your heart is overflowing with love (it is!).

**30** Forgive yourself.

## Orgasms and goals can be fun, but ...

Anne Wilson Schaef has written a great book called *Meditations for Women Who Do Too Much*, in which she suggests that 'Orgasms and goals can be fun, but not if they obliterate everything that goes before.'

First, let's consider this category of women who do too much. Do you belong to it? If so, welcome to the club; you are not alone. We all spend most of our days running to keep up with ourselves, and relaxation is often nothing more than a heavenly fantasy that we might indulge in one day, but not now (we just haven't got the time). I know, you *will* relax but only *later* – on holiday, when everything is finally done, when you retire, in heaven ... So if you can only take a breather *later*, what is it that you are doing now? How many plates are you spinning on sticks? What is the worst thing that could happen if one of them crashed to the ground? The truth is that unless you schedule in your relaxation time you will probably never get to have any. Remember that life coaching brings the fastest results to those who take a calm and relaxed approach – so if you need an excuse to stop, there you have it.

Second, let's think about orgasms and goals! Women do not regard foreplay merely as a means to an end; we feel that intimacy, talking and touching have meaning and importance in themselves. Similarly, in our quest to reach our goals we must remember that the way we choose to get there is as important as the outcome. Goals may come and go, but to experience deep satisfaction and real meaning in your life you need to balance your spiritual awareness of the moment with your material desires for the future. In other words, climb to the top of that mountain but don't forget to enjoy the plants, rocks and people along the way. Get pleasure from the foreplay as well as the orgasm.

## Listen to your inner voice

The super-rational part of you may reject the idea that your instincts or hunches could be giving you useful information. But that inner voice of yours can often bring a new dimension to your understanding of a situation. Think of an occasion when you just 'knew' or sensed something was going to happen ... and then it did! How did you react? Did you dismiss it, thinking it was just a coincidence, or were you aware that you had tapped into your intuitive powers? We feel our spiritual energy as if we are listening to a wise inner voice deep within us. Make no mistake, your intuition is a real and fantastic gift. Use it! The more you tap into this 'knowingness', the stronger the power becomes. And if anyone questions the validity of such a response on the grounds that it is not rational, 'only emotional', you can tell them that this is what makes it so powerful. Hunches, gut reactions and instincts are an incredible source of spiritual and emotional information. They are neither predictable nor reasonable, because they go way beyond anything that logic and rationality can provide.

You use your instincts every day, often without being aware of it. For example, if your partner is feeling stretched, you sense that this is not the right moment to ask him to mend the shelf that's come down in the kitchen. If your boss is out of sorts, you choose another time to ask her for a day off. I know these may seem like ordinary observations, but your inner voice is only an extension of this everyday awareness.

Your inner voice will do whatever it takes to capture your attention. It may come through as a thought that just keeps coming up again and again until you are forced to notice it, or it may manifest as a physical sensation in the pit of your stomach (hence the phrase 'gut instinct'). Alternatively, amazing, inexplicable coincidences may start occurring so that you just have to take note of what is going on. Think back and see if you can identify some of the ways your inner voice has commanded your attention in the past.

New scientific research reveals that a gut reaction really is a physical as well as an emotional response. We have a large knot of nerve cells in our stomachs that can respond to any emotional situation and affect our unconscious decisions. This is why, when these decisions become conscious later on, we are often aware that this is something that we knew all along at a subconscious level.

## Sue and Rob's story

Sue and Rob were desperate to move out of town and leave their high-powered high-stressed jobs. Eventually they agreed that they couldn't afford to take lower paid jobs outside

London, so they found a wonderful house in Surrey and decided to live there and to commute to work.

One morning, as they were in the last stages of negotiating, Sue asked the agent if any new properties had come on the market in the last few days. Rob was surprised because they had agreed to go for the house in Surrey. However, Sue said she had a strong feeling that something else had turned up that she knew they would love. She persuaded the agent to phone into his office to check the latest property information. And sure enough, an interesting new property had come on the market just an hour previously: a house with a craft shop and café attached.

Sue wanted to go and see it. Rob couldn't understand why, as the property was not at all the kind of thing they were after, but Sue persisted, so they drove to see it. It was in a fabulous location in a small village with a good tourist trade. Neither Sue nor Rob had ever thought of running their own business, but when they saw the house even Rob was smitten. Nine months later they were in, and, they say, it's the best thing they have ever done.

Sue says she 'felt' that there was a fantastic opportunity coming for her and Rob, and she just 'knew' something had come on the market on that particular morning that was 'meant' for them. Sue is a very spiritually aware person and has great faith in the power of her hunches and gut reactions. If she connects with a sense of 'knowingness' she always gives her instincts the benefit of the doubt. As a result she has developed an amazing ability to tap into the universal energy flow, as this story clearly demonstrates.

You can't expect this sort of level of awareness immediately but you can begin to develop it. Recognise the different ways that your own inner voice speaks to you. Start to listen out for your intuition. The more you listen, the clearer it will become. Take it slowly at first and follow your hunches in small matters (make that phone call now, read that book …). The more you see the positive results, the more you will begin to trust your inner voice. And when you next have a big decision to make, don't just take the logical view; think things through rationally and then *feel* them through. Ask yourself such questions as:

- What do my instincts say?
- What do I feel at a physical level?
- What gives me the greatest personal fulfilment?
- What does my heart tell me to do?
- What is the most exciting and thrilling option I can take?

People who balance their rationality with their instincts make well judged and inspired choices. With focus, motivation and inspiration the world is your oyster! Be inspired.

---

## TIME OUT

### FIVE-MINUTE RELAXATION

SIT COMFORTABLY, CLOSE YOUR EYES AND BECOME AWARE OF YOUR BREATHING. AS YOUR MIND FILLS WITH NUMEROUS THOUGHTS, JUST NOTICE THEM AND LET THEM GO. DON'T FOLLOW THEM. (THEY WILL KEEP COMING; YOUR MIND NEVER STOPS.)

---

INSTEAD, COME BACK TO YOUR BREATHING. FOLLOW YOUR IN-BREATHS AND OUT-BREATHS: IN AND OUT, IN AND OUT ... AND AS YOU DO SO, START TO BECOME AWARE OF YOUR BODY.

NOW IMAGINE THAT YOUR WHOLE BODY IS RELAXING. BEGIN WITH YOUR TOES AND FEEL A GREAT WAVE OF RELAXATION SWEEPING THROUGH YOUR FEET, CALVES AND THIGHS. YOU CAN FEEL YOUR LEGS GETTING HEAVIER AND HEAVIER. LET THIS CALM AND RELAXED FEELING TRAVEL UP INTO YOUR ABDOMEN AND LOWER BACK. FEEL THE WARM PEACEFUL ENERGY MOVE INTO YOUR CHEST, UPPER BACK AND SHOULDERS. LET YOUR SHOULDERS GO. FEEL YOUR BODY HEAVY, WARM, RELAXED AND PEACEFUL.

NOW LET GO OF ALL TENSION IN YOUR HANDS, ARMS, NECK HEAD AND FACE. YOUR FACIAL MUSCLES LET GO AND YOUR JAWS AND EYES FEEL HEAVY AND RELAXED.

YOU ARE NOW COMPLETELY COMFORTABLE AND AT EASE. A WONDERFUL FEELING OF PEACE AND SERENITY SURROUNDS YOU. ENJOY!

WHEN YOU ARE READY, COME BACK SLOWLY INTO THE ROOM.

THIS IS A GREAT ROUTINE FOR ANY TIME WHEN YOU NEED TO LET GO OF THE STRESSES AND STRAINS OF THE DAY.

# Step 6
# Act Now

*Whatever you can do or dream you can, begin it. Boldness has genius, power and magic in it. Begin it now.*

JOHANN WOLFGANG VON GOETHE

You bought this book because you know that fortune really does favour the brave. In other words, you are aware that you only ever get out what you put in, and that if you want to take charge of your life you must take the responsibility that goes with this.

The blamers and complainers of the world create a neat self-fulfilling prophecy that goes like this: they maintain the attitude that they are always being victimised, that nothing ever goes right for them and that they are bound to lose, and so they believe that it's not worth making any effort to change. Victims are afraid of life and give away their power to others. This means they never have to take a risk, overcome obstacles or make a decision and stand by it. We have all acted in this way at some time in our lives, often when we are facing self-doubt. It's always easy to find something or someone to complain about or blame, and then we can justify hiding away for a while in inactivity (it's all so terrible, there's nothing I can do, it's her fault, oh poor me). But of course this approach will never bring us the life of our dreams.

The first time I recognised and understood the concept of being a victim was when I was in my early thirties. I was in Glastonbury at a self-development workshop run by an amazing shamanistic healer called Maggie Chalmers. In those days I was developing my interest in all things alternative and the powerful mystical energy of Glastonbury drew me like a magnet. However, my 'healing' that day came in a very ordinary way (as big changes usually do). Sue, one of the workshop participants, said something critical to me and I responded by saying that I knew she had never liked me and that she always treated me badly. This was probably very true, but the significance of the occasion lay in what she said next: 'Oh poor you! Always playing the victim, aren't you?' And that was it! I can't remember what happened next, but that moment has stayed with me ever since. Gradually over the next few months I kept noticing where I was acting the victim role. It was like taking a blindfold off and seeing clearly for the first time. This wasn't a comfortable space to be in, but it taught me a huge lesson about myself. Eventually my interest in how to stop being a victim led me to write my first book, on self-esteem. So, Sue, thanks for the challenge. You were absolutely right.

Whenever you feel a 'blame' thought setting in, just stop and check out what's happening. We all fall into this trap sometimes (especially when the going gets extra rough). Notice it and stop it! Remember that every time you blame someone or something, you are giving your power away. If it's 'all their fault' or 'nothing ever goes right' for you, then you will have to wait for whoever or whatever it is to change! Take back your power. You can change any aspect of your life. You can also decide to walk away from victimisers! Choose to take an assertive approach and stand out from the crowd.

# Assertiveness quiz*

Choose answers A or B and see how assertive you are.

**1** A relative rings when you are rushed off your feet and you don't want to talk.

   A  You take the phone call but feel pressurised and hassled.

   B  You say that you can't speak at the moment but that you will ring back when you can.

**2** You have been invited to a dinner party. You have eaten half the meal and you are full.

   A  You carry on eating to please the hosts although you feel uncomfortable.

   B  You stop eating and explain that although the meal was delicious you can't eat any more.

**3** Your doctor prescribes medication for what you thought was a minor complaint.

   A  You just take the pills.

   B  You ask what the pills are for, how they work and if they are going to have any side-effects. If you are unhappy with the answers, you don't take the pills and/or you seek a second opinion.

**4** Your boyfriend drops his stuff all around the house.

   A  You pick it up.

   B  You tell him to get his act together and that you are not his mother!

**5** A double glazing salesperson rings at 7 pm, just as you are about to eat.

   A  You listen to his patter and your dinner goes cold.

*Adapted from my book, *The Self-Esteem Workbook*

B  You tell him you are not interested and put the phone down.

**6** You have just given up smoking and a friend is trying to persuade you to have a cigarette for old time's sake.

A  You can't say no and take one.

B  You say no and leave immediately if you are feeling tempted.

**7** You are invited to a party. You don't like the host/hostess and feel pressurised to buy them a gift even if you don't attend.

A  You resentfully buy a present.

B  You politely apologise for not going and you don't buy a gift.

**8** You believe that you have been overcharged by your solicitor.

A  You just pay up to avoid a scene.

B  You query the bill.

**9** You have taken on too much and can't fit in all that you have promised to do.

A  You become irritated, resentful and angry, and try to do a little bit of everything, ending up making a bad job of the lot.

B  You delegate and find some time to relax.

**10** You are coming home from a party and your partner is over the limit but insists on driving.

A  You get into the passenger seat and worry.

B  You insist that you drive or call a taxi.

**11** You have bought an expensive designer coat and your partner doesn't like it.

A  You don't wear it any more.

B  You like it and so you are going to wear it.

**12** You are seriously trying to lose weight and are out with a crowd who are trying to persuade you to eat a Chinese takeaway with them.

    A  You feel silly about your diet and 'go along' with the others.

    B  You say that you don't want to break your diet and you go home if it gets too difficult.

**13** Your boss asks you to work late when you have an important date arranged.

    A  You cancel your own arrangements and work.

    B  You tell your boss that you have a date you don't want to break and that you don't mind working late sometimes but you need advance warning.

**14** You have booked a table at a restaurant, but when you arrive you find it's next to the toilet.

    A  You swallow your disappointment and make the best of the situation.

    B  You ask to be moved, and, if there's nowhere else to sit, you go to another restaurant.

**15** You decide on the spur of the moment to go out for the evening because you really need a break. A friend calls and asks if you will go round and babysit.

    A  You ditch your own plans because it's too difficult to say no.

    B  You tell her you're sorry but you have already made arrangements to go out.

Score 1 for each time you answered A. Score 2 for each time you answered B.

## If you scored  15–19:

You find it hard to stand up for yourself and usually put others' needs before your own. This can lead you to feel resentful and put upon, and you might find yourself feeling surprisingly angry on occasions. You act passively rather than assertively and it is probably hard for you to express your true feelings. It is often difficult for you to make clear decisions and you find it very hard to say no to people.

## If you scored  20–24:

You know how to act assertively but sometimes it's just too much of a challenge to put yourself first. Although you are aware that you are behaving passively at times, you sometimes let yourself fall into the trap of worrying about what other people think. You would like to be able to say what you really think and feel more often.

## If you scored  25–30:

You are an assertive person and you know it! You have developed some strategies that allow you take charge in any situation and you can say no without feeling guilty. Your high score is a reflection of your confidence and self-esteem. Congratulations, you stand out from the crowd!

---

# Give and take

How did you do? Don't worry if you are inclined to be a 'people pleaser' some of the time; we all like to be liked and this can lead us into victim-type behaviour. You might find it easy to be assertive at work and yet be a doormat in relationships. Perhaps you act confidently when you are in a familiar situation but fall apart when faced with a new scenario. And what is the difference between being a thoughtful and kind person and being a pushover? If you cancel a hot date in order to help a friend, are you being a good mate or are you just a victim who can't say no? It can be hard to decide. Think of a time when you put someone else's needs before your own and felt OK about it. Now remember when you put your plans on hold for another person and then felt angry and resentful. This is how you work out the difference between being a caring person and being a victim; you check how you feel.

If you act the way you do because you are feeling afraid/angry/intimidated/helpless/irritated ... (or any other negative emotion) you are acting like a victim. Victims never win the big prizes, in fact they never win anything. In life coaching we recognise the absolute need for assertive and positive action if we are to bring about the changes we desire. How can you go for your goals with that 100 per cent self-belief if you are trying to keep everyone happy all of the time?

Reaching for your best means just that. It means not selling yourself short or doing anything you really don't want to do or building your whole life around the needs of others. Of course, you live and work with other people and compromises are often necessary. Life is all about give and take – just make sure you're not giving the whole time!

## QUICK TIP

WHEN YOU WANT TO SAY NO AND YOU ARE STRUGGLING TO SAY IT, STOP FOR A SECOND AND GIVE THE PERSON YOU ARE SPEAKING TO A HUGE SMILE. NOW BOTH OF YOU CAN RELAX AND THE ATMOSPHERE WILL FEEL LESS TENSE.

- YES, YOU CAN BE A GOOD FRIEND AND STILL SAY NO.

- YOU CAN BE A GOOD WORKER AND SAY NO.

- YOU CAN BE A GOOD LOVER AND SAY NO.

- YOU CAN BE A GOOD PARENT AND SAY NO.

LIGHTEN UP AND JUST SAY NO WHEN YOU NEED TO. IF THE PERSON CAN'T TAKE IT GRACEFULLY, THEN ASK YOURSELF WHY THEY ARE NOT RESPONSIVE TO YOUR NEEDS.

SAYING NO IS EASY, AND PRACTICE MAKES PERFECT.

## My story

My career as a self-help writer, life coach, therapist and counsellor really began on the day I came face to face with my own self-pity at that Glastonbury workshop. Although I had everything going for me: a good start in life with positive and supportive parents, a university education and plenty of friends, I still felt low in self-confidence and attracted poor intimate relationships. I am telling you this because I think it's important to know that everyone struggles with their negative patterns at some point in their life. No one is born 100 per cent positive; we all face self-doubt and we all have to learn to transform negative energy if we are going to make the very best of ourselves and lead a successful and fulfilling life.

When I married my first husband and had two children very close together, I quickly fell into a resigned and martyrish role as wife and mother. Of course, early motherhood is challenging and we have to put our children's needs first, but I took this to the extreme. I lost all sense of myself and of my own needs, and I also lost the confidence to know what I wanted and how to go for it. I changed from a positive person into a lost soul who had forgotten how to stand up for herself. I loved my mothering role and it gave me a sense of identity, but this could never be enough in itself. My husband was running his own business and was away a lot, and I felt stuck at home and fed up. The marriage ended and I left with the children. Suddenly there was no one to blame and so I just had to get on with it.

When you have to get it together, of course you do. My spirit came back and I turned myself around. I discovered many of the techniques that you are reading about in this book and I put them to use. Believe me, they do work! I changed the way I related to partners and eventually I met and married a wonderful man and had another child. My great desire to change developed into a fascination with self-help techniques, and I applied these tools to developing my career.

I would never suggest that you use any strategy that I have not found effective myself. I believe that if they work for me, they can certainly work for you too. So use the 7 Steps in this book, do the exercises and try the techniques. Be aware that you won't always get everything right but that you are always doing your best. When you think a 'blame' thought and start to feel sorry for yourself, remember that *you are in control* of your destiny. Take charge of your life and take positive action and you will accomplish whatever you set out to achieve.

Every time you challenge your own victim-like behaviour, you will come closer to being the real you. The real you knows who she is and what she wants (and doesn't want); she is not afraid to stand up for her rights or to express her needs and she does this with style and grace. You deserve the best and you are determined and focused, so smile and step forward into your own power, NOW!

## Learn to surf

There is a wonderful poster of 70-something yogi Swami Satchitananda (with flowing robes and long white beard) riding a surfboard on top of the waves in Hawaii. The caption says: 'You can't stop the waves but you can learn to surf.' What a great image this is.

The truth is that stress is part of life; someone or something is always challenging us, but this doesn't mean we have to go down each time and become the victims of circumstance and other people's behaviour. You can negotiate the ups and downs by being true to yourself and being positive in your outlook and actions. There is no need to get sucked under those waves when you can just ride them easily and effortlessly. The way to keep focused and moving forward towards your objectives (regardless of the distractions and obstacles that you meet) is to take affirmative action towards your goals every day. Let positive action become an everyday habit and then whatever life throws your way you can still keep your eye on your target and move persistently towards it. Try repeating the following positive affirmations. They will give you the energy and bounce to surf the waves and stay on top, however bumpy the ride.

- I deserve the best that life can give me.
- Every day I move closer to my goals.
- I know how to get what I want.
- I trust myself.
- I am a winner.
- The universe supports my every move.
- I am safe.
- I create my own life.

---

## TIME OUT

RELAX AND IMAGINE YOURSELF IN THE SEA OFF THAT HAWAIIAN BEACH. THE SUN IS HOT, THE SKY IS BLUE, THE SAND IS SILVER-WHITE AND YOU ARE RIDING THE WAVES. AS YOU SURF ALONG, WITH THE COOL SPRAY HITTING YOUR BODY, IT ALL FEELS SO EASY AND RELAXED AND SO MUCH FUN.

STAY WITH THIS FEELING AS YOU CONSIDER ANY SITUATION IN YOUR LIFE WHERE YOU ARE BEGINNING TO 'GO UNDER' IN SOME WAY. YOU KNOW THAT YOU CAN RISE ABOVE THIS, SO PICTURE YOURSELF SURFING ANY TROUBLESOME WAVES IN YOUR LIFE. SEE HOW EASY IT IS TO STAY ON TOP AND FEEL THE JOY AS YOU BALANCE ON YOUR SURFBOARD, CUTTING THROUGH THE WATER EASILY AND GRACEFULLY.

RECREATE THIS IMAGE WHENEVER THE SEAS OF LIFE START TO TROUBLE YOU. KNOW THAT YOU ARE A GREAT SURFER AND THAT YOU CAN ALWAYS STAY ON TOP.

---

# Following through

Your reputation goes before you. If you are known as a decisive go-getting sort of person, then others will be inclined to take you and your plans more seriously. More seriously that is than they will take someone who dithers and twitters around in a whirlpool of uncertainty. Here we get to the very heart of positive assertive action: to achieve your goal you must be committed and ready to make the decisions that will ultimately lead to your success. There are always two choices:

1  NO COMMITMENT = NO RISK = NO DECISION =
   NO PLAN = NO GOAL
2  COMMITMENT = READY TO TAKE A CHANCE =
   DECISION = PLAN = GOAL

If you take choice number one you are choosing not to follow through. This is OK as long as you are aware that you have made this choice, but if you do it unconsciously, you may end up thinking that things didn't come together because you are a victim of circumstance (things never go your way, you are a born loser etc., etc.). If you are in any situation where you are feeling out of control and in a mess, just check: did you take choice number one?

This is the difference between people who 'can't do' and people who can. Negative thinkers keep all their options closed because they don't believe they can come through for themselves. Positive thinkers can always come through with a plan, however difficult their circumstances.

When I was running a career-counselling project in Cornwall I had two clients who wanted to apply for the same job. John was a graduate who had never worked; he was articulate and bright and looked very presentable. Emily had flunked her A levels and had done any job to make ends meet for the last three years; she was funny and clever and *longing* to get a proper job at last. The job they were applying for was as a support worker for a project working with people with learning difficulties.

I worked with them both separately on their application forms and went through the usual interview technique procedure, and I thought they were both good candidates. Neither of them got the job, but at the interview they were told about a volunteer programme that the project was running.

John came away angry and disappointed that he hadn't been given a job that he was 'overqualified for' (his words), and he was furious that it was suggested he might do volunteer work (even though he was unemployed at the time).

Emily was disappointed as well, because she had been very enthusiastic about the project and felt that she would really have fitted in. Although she was working during the day, Emily signed up for the volunteer programme so that she could 'at least be a part of it in some way' (her words). She worked for nothing three evenings a week for six months and decided that come what may she wanted a career in this area. Of course, her dedication and commitment paid off when a similar job came up working for another agency; she had the experience and had demonstrated her commitment to this sort of work and she got the job. She went to college on day release for two years and now she is a qualified project worker.

John remained unemployed and fell into a cycle of depression. The last time I saw him he told me his problem was that he was overqualified and that employers were intimidated by him. Since when did a university degree become such a hindrance?

The moral of this story is: no commitment, no focus and no

decision lead to absolutely nowhere, while commitment, focus, and decisions lead to goal achievement.

# How to be decisive

When you're on a high it's easy to get clear and make good focused decisions. On a less good day it can be quite hard. Use this exercise on such a day.

## Step 1: Discover your intention

Whether you are trying to make a big or a small decision, the process is always the same. You can't act if you can't decide how to act, and you can't make a decision unless you know what you intend to happen. To discover your intention ask yourself this question: 'What do I want to happen?' This is a powerful and assertive question, because as soon as you identify your intention you create a laser-like focus that clarifies your decision-making process and points directly to the action you need to take.

- Take any area of your life where you would welcome change.
- Discover your intention.
- Write down your answers – be as specific as you can be.

## Step 2: Clarify your decisions

Now ask yourself, 'How do I make this happen?' Brainstorm for ideas and write down everything that comes up, however unconnected and inappropriate it may seem. Spend some time on this and maybe go back to it later to see if you can come up with anything else. See this as a creative and non-pressurised task and you will be surprised by your ideas. Use your findings to help you decide exactly how you need to change your behaviour.

### Step 3: Take action

You have to change your behaviour if you are looking for a new result. Do what you always do and you will be stuck with what you always get.

- Visualise your intention – really see and experience your outcome in action.
- Affirm that your outcome is happening – believe 100 per cent in your goal.
- Take new and appropriate action.

Henry was being bullied by his manager at work. He liked his job but wanted to take control of the situation. We worked together, using the exercise you have just done, and this is what Henry's plan looked like:

### Step 1: Intention

To keep my job. This means that my relationship with my manager must change.

### Step 2: Decisions

To demonstrate that I won't tolerate being treated so badly.
To stand up for myself.
To stop being afraid of authority figures.

### Step 3: Action

To communicate more clearly by saying what I mean and standing by it. To stop saying yes when I really mean no.
To be more assertive at work and to take a few calculated risks (there's nothing to lose, things can't get much worse).
To leave my job if my new approach doesn't work. I'm not staying anywhere where I'm not treated with respect.

You can see how effective this exercise can be; it can take you from muddle and indecision into a clear vision of what you want and how to get it. Never underestimate the power of writing down your thoughts, feelings and goals. When you get things down on paper, they seem clearer and more accessible, so keep writing in your notebook.

---

By now you are probably feeling enthusiastic and motivated and more confident about making changes in your life. Indeed, you may already have started! Positive action, just like positive thinking, will become second nature to you if you practise it. Whatever thoughts and actions you repeat will eventually become your routine behaviours. Whatever you turn your attention to will develop and grow, so why not choose to reinforce your highest and clearest vision of yourself. We run our lives according to our habitual patterns of thinking, feeling and behaving, but we are always free to make new fresh choices if the old habits aren't working. Change your behaviour patterns; choose positive, direct action and step into your power. You are bigger and bolder than you think you are. Act now.

---

## TIME OUT

### FIVE-MINUTE RELAXATION

TAKE A WELL DESERVED BREAK. KICK OFF YOUR SHOES AND RELAX COMPLETELY AND UTTERLY. CLOSE YOUR EYES, SLOW DOWN YOUR BREATHING, LET GO OF ALL CONCERNS AND ENJOY THIS WONDERFUL, RELAXING AND CALMING VISUALISATION.

IMAGINE A BEAUTIFUL OUTDOOR SETTING. STEP RIGHT INTO THE SCENE AND SEE YOURSELF STROLLING ALONG A WHITE PATH TOWARDS A BEAUTIFUL CRYSTALLINE FOUNTAIN THAT YOU CAN SEE IN THE DISTANCE.

---

AS YOU GET CLOSER, YOU SEE THAT THIS IS A MAGICAL HEALING FOUNTAIN OF WHITE LIGHT, WHICH CAN ENERGISE AND INVIGORATE YOU.

AS YOU STEP INTO THIS FOUNTAIN, YOU SEE LARGE DROPS OF WHITE LIGHT CASCADING OVER YOU. YOU FEEL THE LIGHT ENERGY ENVELOP AND EMBRACE YOU. THEN YOU SEE THIS WHITE LIGHT TURNING INTO THE SPECTRUM OF RAINBOW COLOURS. LET THE CASCADE CHANGE TO YOUR FAVOURITE COLOUR. FEEL THE HEALING QUALITIES OF THE COLOUR SURROUND YOU AND INFUSE EVERY CELL OF YOUR BEING. EXPERIENCE YOURSELF RADIATING THIS COLOUR.

PLAY IN THIS FOUNTAIN FOR AS LONG AS YOU LIKE. CHANGE THE COLOURS AND FEEL THE DIFFERENCE IN EACH ONE. EVERY COLOUR HAS ITS OWN SPECIAL HEALING QUALITIES.

WHEN YOU ARE READY, STEP OUT FROM THE FOUNTAIN AND TAKE THE PATH HOME. GIVE THANKS FOR A WONDERFUL EXPERIENCE AND REMEMBER THAT YOU CAN RECREATE THIS FOUNTAIN AT ANY TIME AND IN ANY PLACE FOR A RELAXING AND REFRESHING BREAK.

# Step 7
# Take Control

*One of the marks of an intelligent person is to be able to distinguish what is worth doing and what isn't and to be able to set priorities.*

A NN  W ILSON  S CHAEF

Are you:

- Feeling stuck in a rut that you can't think yourself out of however positive you try to be?
- Busy rushing around getting nowhere fast?
- Surrounded by chaos?
- Trying to beat the clock?
- Putting off some important activity that is vital to your progress?

If you are doing any of these things, you need to bring some simple order to your days. Time-wasting, procrastinating and rushing are all problems that can easily be resolved by simplifying and restructuring your daily allocation of 24 hours. Simple lifestyle changes really can make all the difference to whether you can find the energy, space and commitment to go for your goals. Time is always on your side if you work with it instead of against it.

When you are motivated, inspired, focused on your goals and ready to act assertively all you need to do is to get organised. Don't worry; this is much easier than it sounds. Clients often groan when I talk about organisation, because they think it sounds too much like hard work. But in fact the opposite is true. Life feels like hard work when you get to the end of the day only to find that you haven't achieved anything that really matters, or when you can't get your exciting new goal off the ground because you just don't seem to have the time. It's only too easy to get distracted when you are faced with an unspecified 'to do' list; the hours can drift away and yet another day passes in which you didn't take a step towards bringing even one of your dreams closer to reality. You will begin to lose confidence in your wonderful plans and ideas if you don't start to activate them. Taking control means making sure you have the time to take positive steps towards your specified goals.

## Take the pressure off

How does it feel when you are in the middle of your juggling act and the balls start to fall? Do you panic and try to move even faster to make up for lost time? Of course you do. We have all been there. But speeding up doesn't resolve anything. As soon as we start fighting time we put ourselves in an all-lose situation. The principles of *Weekend Life Coach* are based on the fact that winning ways depend upon a balanced mixture of focus and relaxation, so let's apply this philosophy here.

One of the easiest ways to get things done efficiently and enjoyably is to start to think differently about any task that you are doing. Think of a job that needs doing. Now how do you feel? Are you delighted and energised by the prospect or do you feel pressurised and stressed? Can you feel your energy levels going up or going down? It's not hard to see that the more delighted you feel to do something, the more likely it is that you will be able to accomplish it in a relaxed, focused and efficient way. Notice what happens when you say to yourself, 'I've got to this' or 'I should do that' or 'I must do the other'; your energy drops through the floor and you feel reluctant to get going. This is when you can come up with all those reasons not to do something (too busy, too tired, no time ...).

However, if you turn your attitude around and say to yourself 'I'm happy to do this', you will discover a new spring in your step. Create an eager mood and you will find yourself invigorated by a fresh new wave of 'can do' energy. I tell my clients to fall in love with their goals. This is a terrific tip. Get passionate about them, keep thinking how wonderful they are, adore the prospect of achieving them, and the rest is easy. When you are super-thrilled (or even just plain happy) to do whatever it is you have to do, you will lighten your load and enliven your energy.

## Save time

Yes, you really can save time! When you get down to analysing your day, you will be amazed to discover how much time you waste on things that don't give you any reward. In life coaching we talk about the 80/20 rule. This rule reminds us to make good choices about where to put our time and energy. It says that 20 per cent of our activities will be likely to create 80 per cent of the significant achievements in our life. Life coach Carole Gaskell calls this focused 20 per cent our 'gold time' activities. You can recognise your own gold activities by naming the top three things you need to do to bring your goals into reality. Stop wasting time and losing energy on non-productive and unfocused tasks and concentrate instead on these gold activities.

## 10 ways to save time

1 Cut the time you spend on minor tasks and devote the time you gain to more valuable activities.

If you carry your 'to do' list in your head, you are likely to get lost in trivial pursuits and lose track of the main game. Get into the habit of writing down your top daily priorities and keep checking this list to ensure that you are dealing with them. This will stop you getting distracted and enable you to achieve much more.

2 Cut the time you spend procrastinating and devote the time you gain to getting on with it!

Those old excuses that keep coming up to convince you that it's OK to postpone that activity once again are soul-destroying and will rob you of your self-respect. If you are constantly putting something off, check out your reasons. If you know you will never do it, then let it go completely. Don't even think about it again. And if it's something that has to be done, then do it as soon as possible. I promise you, you will feel fabulous afterwards!

3 Cut the time you spend dwelling on your inadequacies and devote the time you gain to concentrating on your strengths.

The more you think about something, the bigger it gets. Forget about what you can't do and focus on what you can. And if something is really beyond you, find someone else to do the job.

4 Cut the time you spend trying to be perfect and devote the time you gain to doing something entirely

relaxing and self-indulgent (scented bath, sauna, facial, swim, sleep … you name it!).

Perfectionists spend too much time trying to be 'good enough'. If this is you, do the following: give it your best shot and then drop it. Your best is always enough.

5 Cut the time you spend worrying and devote the time you gain to problem-solving.

Take that worry and face it. There's no point letting it drag you down until you are fit for nothing. Decide whether you can do anything to resolve it. If you can, then do it. And if you can't, then let it go.

6 Cut the time you spend doubting yourself and devote the time you gain to believing in yourself.

Most of our time-wasting is a consequence of our doubts and fears. Use positive mantras to overcome this negativity. Whenever you are feeling stuck, remember to say to yourself, 'I can do this.' Very soon you will believe it to be true (because of course it is!).

7 Cut the time you spend acting unconsciously and devote the time you gain to developing awareness.

If you act with awareness, you won't have to pay for your mistakes in the future. Every action has a consequence and everything that is happening to you right now is linked to things that you chose to do (or not to do) in the past. Know that whatever you do today will have significance further down the line. Every action you take is a seed that will bloom for you in the future, so choose your seeds carefully and create a positive reality.

8 Cut the time you spend wondering what people are thinking about you and devote the time you save to pleasing yourself.

You can't please all of the people all of the time, so stop trying. If you value someone's opinion, then by all means listen to them, and if you don't, then why care?

9 Cut the time you spend dwelling on the past and worrying about the future and devote the time you save to making a go of it now.

Don't let remorse and guilt hold you back. If you did something that you regret, then make amends if you can; if you can't, then let go of it. If you feel that you missed a chance back then, why not take it now if you can? And stop fretting about what is to come. The past is gone and we don't know what the future holds; all we have is this present moment – live it!

10 Cut the time you spend believing that life can't be fun and devote the time you save to believing that it can be.

People who do too much often think that they can only have fun after the work is done, and that seems to be never (as they keep moving the goalposts). If you ever fall into this trap, try focusing on what you have achieved rather than on what still has to be done. Celebrate your successes every step of the way and your life will become much more fun. Happiness is a state of mind which opens doors to new possibilities and opportunities. Don't forget to enjoy going for your goals.

## Take a reality check

Before we look at more time management skills and how to create efficient action plans, let's take a breather. Better organisation can certainly help us to make the most of our time, but it will not help us if we are behaving like do-aholics. Do-aholics are one step on from workaholics, and in the quest to

# QUICK TIP

GIVE YOURSELF A BOOST OF CONFIDENCE BY TRYING THIS SIMPLE TIP.

THINK OF ALL THE SMALL JOBS YOU KEEP PROMISING YOURSELF YOU WILL DO – NO GREAT PROJECTS HERE, JUST THOSE MODEST TASKS YOU JUST DON'T EVER SEEM TO GET ROUND TO. CHOOSE THINGS SUCH AS, CLEAN OUT THAT DRAWER, WRITE A LETTER TO ..., PHONE ..., SEW A BUTTON ON MY SKIRT, REPOT THAT PLANT, ETC.

MAKE A LIST OF THESE MINOR JOBS.

## THINGS I NEED TO DO

. . . . . . . . . . . . . . . . . . . . . . . . . . . . . . . . . . . . . . . . . . .
. . . . . . . . . . . . . . . . . . . . . . . . . . . . . . . . . . . . . . . . . . .
. . . . . . . . . . . . . . . . . . . . . . . . . . . . . . . . . . . . . . . . . . .

MAKE SURE YOU DO WRITE THEM DOWN, BECAUSE THIS WAY THEY WILL BECOME MORE REAL AND MORE DO-ABLE. NEVER MIND HOW LONG THE LIST IS. NOW CHOOSE *ONE THING* FROM YOUR LIST AND DO IT. DON'T YOU FEEL FANTASTIC?

SOMETIMES WHEN WE PROMISE THAT WE WILL GET SOMETHING TOGETHER AND THEN WE DON'T WE CAN SLIP INTO A NEGATIVE CYCLE OF LOW SELF-RESPECT (FEELING THAT WE CAN'T TRUST OURSELVES TO FOLLOW THROUGH WITH *ANYTHING*). WE OFTEN SPEND MORE TIME AND ENERGY THINKING ABOUT DOING SOMETHING AND THEN NOT DOING IT THAN IT WOULD

ACTUALLY TAKE TO DO IT. BREAK THIS HABIT AND SHOW YOURSELF HOW EASY IT IS TO DO JUST ONE OF YOUR OVERDUE JOBS AND YOU WILL INSTANTLY MOVE INTO A POSITIVELY INSPIRED CYCLE.

NEXT TIME YOU HEAR YOURSELF SAYING, 'I REALLY NEED TO ... JUST GO AHEAD AND DO IT!

'have it all' it's easy to become addicted in this way. If you are feeling too busy to be happy, check your lifestyle. If you are 'doing it all' then ask yourself why. We will come back to this when we look at your work/life balance in Section 2. Meanwhile start to notice the times when you feel as if you are on a fast train going nowhere.

Order and plans will not make your life easier if you just fill in your newly freed up time with even more tasks. Keep things in perspective by taking a reality check every now and again. Ask yourself, 'Is this one plan too many?' And if it is, just stop, slow down and enjoy the moment. However wonderful the goal, it is never worth it if you have to sacrifice the quality of your life.

As a barrister, mother of four, charity worker and the Prime Minister's wife, Cherie Blair seemed to epitomise the perfect modern woman – organised, flexible and in control. But during the row over her connection with convicted conman Peter Foster, she made an emotional statement to the press which revealed that the pressure to keep everything together all the time was just too great: 'I am juggling a lot of balls ... Sometimes some of the balls get dropped. I am not super-woman ... There are not enough hours in the day.'

So Cherie has come clean and admitted what all of us knew all along: no one can do it all and have it all (even if they have personal assistants, nannies, stylists, domestic help and so on). A recent survey by a top UK health magazine and health insurers BUPA found that women are sick and tired of so-called superwoman role models. So let's all get real about what, why and how much we are doing. Be warned, whenever you do too much, something has to crack, and that will usually be you. It's a delicate balancing act: overstep the line and 'control' quickly slips into 'out of control'.

---

## TIME OUT

TRY THIS SIMPLE YOGA TECHNIQUE, WHICH WILL HELP YOU TO REDUCE YOUR STRESS LEVELS AND INCREASE YOUR ENERGY.

SIT ON A CHAIR OR CROSS-LEGGED ON THE FLOOR AND PLACE YOUR HANDS ON YOUR KNEES. CLOSE YOUR EYES AND SLOW DOWN YOUR BREATHING.

WHEN YOU ARE READY, INHALE THROUGH YOUR NOSE AND ARCH YOUR SPINE INWARDS SO THAT YOUR CHEST IS PUSHED OUT. EXHALE AND SLUMP YOUR SHOULDERS FORWARDS AND DOWN SO THAT YOUR SPINE IS COMPLETELY RELAXED.

REPEAT 10 TIMES, MAINTAINING A COMFORTABLE RHYTHM.

---

# The activity spectrum

Wise use of time always comes down to a question of balance. When clients tell me they feel out of control of their life, I know they are operating at one or the other end of the activity spectrum: they are either doing too little or doing too much. The following diagram shows the three possible paths of activity: underdoing, overdoing and balanced action.

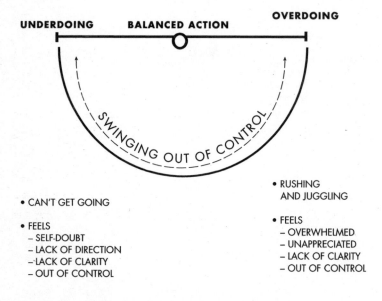

- CAN'T GET GOING

- FEELS
  – SELF-DOUBT
  – LACK OF DIRECTION
  – LACK OF CLARITY
  – OUT OF CONTROL

- RUSHING AND JUGGLING

- FEELS
  – OVERWHELMED
  – UNAPPRECIATED
  – LACK OF CLARITY
  – OUT OF CONTROL

**SWINGING OUT OF CONTROL**

Underdoing is characterised by a feeling of being stuck, being unable to act and not knowing which way to turn. You can sometimes find yourself in this state when you have taken a blow to your confidence and are feeling the demons of self-doubt. We have all experienced this at some time or other. The way out is to get absolutely clear about what you want to happen and how to set it in motion.

Overdoing is also a symptom of lack of focus, as you rush from pillar to post and back again, struggling to fulfil impossible demands and trying to keep everyone happy. If you juggle too many projects, it will always end in tears (with you feeling unappreciated, resentful, overworked and out of control).

Sometimes you may find yourself swinging from underdoing to overdoing in an attempt to get out of your rut and get going. This won't work. Before long you will find yourself swinging back exhaustedly into a state of inaction.

The only way to feel in control and to achieve real success is to take this middle path of balanced action. Take a look at the activity spectrum table and you will see that this route begins with mental clarity and then leads on to the creation and fulfilment of realistic plans. This is the only way to move forward. When a client says they feel out of control I always begin by looking at ways in which they can clean up their lives, so that they can create time and space to think things through clearly. This often involves nothing more complicated than some basic de-cluttering techniques to clear the way for physical, mental and emotional changes.

## Get clear

The path of balanced action is the one that leads to success, and it depends on a clear focus. When you can simplify and streamline your life, the paths to your goals become clear. De-cluttering leads to a sense of purposefulness and wellbeing, and as you bring order into your material world this will lead into greater psychological clarity.

Look around your home and work environments. Are they a

# THE ACTIVITY SPECTRUM TABLE

| UNDERDOING | BALANCED ACTION | OVERDOING |
|:---:|:---:|:---:|
| LACK OF MENTAL CLARITY | CLEAR FOCUS | LACK OF MENTAL CLARITY |
| ▼ | ▼ | ▼ |
| TOO FEW REAL PLANS | REALISTIC PLANS | TOO MANY PLANS |
| ▼ | ▼ | ▼ |
| INACTIVITY | USEFUL ACTIVITY | OVERACTIVITY |
| ▼ | ▼ | ▼ |
| NO TIME FRAME FOR ACHIEVEMENTS | SPECIFIED TIME FRAME | UNREALISTIC TIME FRAME FOR ACHIEVEMENTS |
| ▼ | ▼ | ▼ |
| NO GOALS REACHED | ACCOMPLISHMENT OF GOALS | CHASING TOO MANY GOALS |
| ▼ | ▼ | ▼ |
| LACK OF PERSONAL SATISFACTION | SENSE OF PERSONAL SATISFACTION | LACK OF PERSONAL SATISFACTION |
| ▼ | ▼ | ▼ |
| LOW SELF-RESPECT | HIGH SELF-RESPECT | LOW SELF-RESPECT |
| ▼ | ▼ | ▼ |
| FEELING OUT OF CONTROL | FEELING IN CONTROL | FEELING OUT OF CONTROL |
| ▼ | ▼ | ▼ |
| LOW ENERGY | HIGH ENERGY | LOW ENERGY |
| STRESSED | RELAXED | STRESSED |
| TIRED | ENTHUSIASTIC | FRANTIC |
| NEGATIVE | POSITIVE | NEGATIVE |
| DEPRESSED | UPBEAT | DEPRESSED |

reflection of a person who is organised and in control? Are there piles of 'things that might come in handy' gathering dust in corners? Have you got a junk drawer or cupboard where you put everything that hasn't got a home? Is your clutter weighing you down? You know all about cardboard boxes, municipal dumps and second-hand shops, so get going and do what must be done. De-junking is such a fabulously liberating technique, and creating outer order definitely leads on to a new sense of inner order. Before clients can take the path of balanced action they often feel the need to spring clean their life. When they do this they feel more in control, both physically and emotionally. Look back at the activity spectrum table and you will see that the successful path of balanced action relies on mental clarity.

There is a universal law which states that you cannot let anything new into your life until you have made some space by letting go of the old. This applies at all levels: the physical, mental and emotional. Whenever you hang on to useless items in your environment you are metaphysically hanging on to old patterns and limitations.

## Lucy's story

When Lucy first spoke to me she told me she wanted to change everything in her life. She said that she felt 'just like a teenager' and that her life was stuck in the slow lane. She had a long list of goals but couldn't see how she could create them when she was 'so busy' all the time (stuck and busy: a classic case of swinging out of control).

Lucy was 28 and so certainly qualified as an adult, but an early discussion revealed that her flat was full of memorabilia from her childhood. Her wardrobe was full to the brim with clothes that were one or even two sizes too small for her;

some were from her teenage years and others were intended for an unspecified time when she would have lost enough weight to fit into them. So Lucy was stuck in two worlds: somewhere in the past with clothes she had outgrown, and somewhere in the future with clothes she couldn't wear until she lost weight. She felt that the state of her wardrobe somehow epitomised the state of her life and that drastic action was called for.

Lucy asked a friend to help her and give her moral support, and started filling black bags. Although she found it 'very scary' to start with, she soon got into it. She threw away or gave to a charity shop every single thing that she couldn't wear. This immediately led on to a drastic clean up of her flat and then she redecorated. Six weeks later Lucy had a new job and a new boyfriend (and new clothes that fitted her).

Think about what you are holding on to and why. Go and clear up one small corner of debris in your life right now. You will feel liberated and cleansed, and who knows where it may lead?

## Time management and action plans

As you reach for your goals you will want to make the very best use of your time. But many clients cringe at the mention of wall planners, diaries, pinboards, lists and the rest; there seems to be a natural reluctance to committing in this way. If you are about to skip this section, then you are probably just the sort of person who needs to structure her time. Planning your time is an easy task; you just need to begin. Writing things down, making lists and referring to your diary or wall-planner will help you to prioritise tasks (very important) and to delete jobs that don't really have to be done. Research

# QUICK TIP

- CAN YOU THINK OF SOMETHING THAT IS DISTRACTING YOU OR DRAINING YOUR ENERGY OR GETTING ON YOUR NERVES AT THE MOMENT? ARE THERE ANY ENERGY VAMPIRES IN YOUR LIFE? IF THERE ARE, YOU WILL KNOW WHAT OR WHO THEY ARE.

- DO YOU HAVE TO PUT UP WITH ANYTHING OR ANYBODY THAT ANNOYS YOU AND STOPS YOU MOVING FORWARD IN THE IMPORTANT AREAS OF YOUR LIFE? SUCH ENERGY DRAINERS COULD INCLUDE DOMESTIC APPLIANCES THAT AREN'T WORKING PROPERLY, UNFINISHED PROJECTS, OVER-DEMANDING ACQUAINTANCES, DIRTY CLOTHES CONTINUALLY DUMPED ON THE FLOOR, NEGATIVE FAMILY MEMBERS, UNRELIABLE CO-WORKERS, A DISORGANISED DESK ... YOU NAME IT.

- MAKE A LIST OF YOUR ANNOYANCES (PETTY AND NOT SO PETTY). NOW TAKE YOUR TOP THREE IRRITATIONS, CHOOSE ONE AND DECIDE TO DO SOMETHING ABOUT IT.

- GO BACK TO YOUR LIST, PRIORITISE THE ITEMS (MOST ANNOYING AT THE TOP) AND START TO DEAL WITH THEM, WORKING YOUR WAY METHODICALLY DOWN THE LIST. WHEN A NEW 'VAMPIRE' ARISES, JUST ADD IT TO YOUR LIST. YOU WILL FEEL MUCH BETTER BECAUSE YOU WILL KNOW THAT THESE IRRITATIONS ARE UNDER CONTROL AND THAT THEY WILL BE DEALT WITH SOON.

shows that written goals and plans have much more chance of happening than those we just think and talk about. We take them more seriously when we get them down on paper. Add a few of the strategies we have already mentioned, such as putting an end to procrastination and dealing with energy drainers, and you will suddenly find yourself with time to spare. Effective time management puts a real value on your time and effort and this will do wonders for your confidence and self-worth. Other people in your life will also be affected and you will notice them treating you with more respect.

When you can manage your time you can create effective action plans and this, of course, is vital if you are going to achieve your goals. The way you do this is entirely up to you, but here is an example of a good way to go about it.

EXERCISE:

## Make an action plan

Choose one of your short-term goals (achievable in three months or less). Now take a piece of paper and divide it into five columns with the following headings:

INTENTION  METHOD  NEEDS  REVIEW  CHANGES

Fill in the columns in the following way:

INTENTION: State your goal: *I want to* . . . . . . . . . . . . . . . . . . .

METHOD: List your action steps in order: *The specific action steps I need to take are* . . . . . . . . . . . . . . . . . . . . . . . . . . . . . . . . . .

NEEDS: List all the resources you may need, for example, help, professional advice, family support ... This list may alter as time passes.

REVIEW:  Give yourself some realistic deadlines. Decide on certain dates at which to assess your progress.

CHANGES: Note any changes that occur. This is your flexibility column and will affect the rest of your plan. Be ready to adapt your plan so that you can respond creatively to change instead of being floored by the first setback.

Once you have achieved a short-term goal you will be inspired to plan for more ambitious and far-reaching ones. You can use exactly the same procedure for a long-term goal. Let your plan be specific but also flexible (a focused and relaxed approach is the way to success). Tick off the action steps as you achieve them and make sure you celebrate each and every step forward.

You will take the pressure off yourself by choosing to take control of your life. Planning is easy and it will lead to your success. Make time work for you and you will be amazed by what you can achieve. Take control.

---

# TIME OUT

## FIVE-MINUTE RELAXATION

Create a relaxing spa in your bathroom. Be warned, this relaxation might easily extend to 20 minutes, as it's so enjoyable!

- Burn scented candles and turn off all the lights. Use an essential oil burner if you have one.

- Use your favourite bath products (fragrances, bubbles, salts and so on).

- Sprinkle a few drops of your favourite scented oil onto a warm, damp flannel and lay it on your forehead while you soak.

- Have some large fluffy towels warming on the radiator, ready for when you are finished.

- Wrap yourself up in the towels and lie down and relax when your bath is over. Sip your favourite herb tea from a wine glass.

- Relax, relax, relax.

# Part Two

# GET THE LIFE YOU WANT

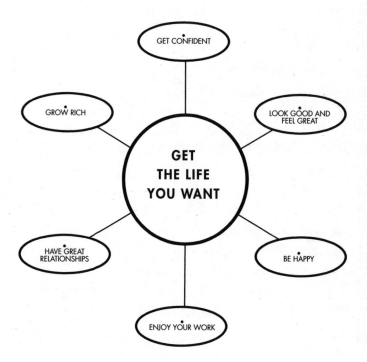

# Get Confident

*Physical beauty is ephemeral, but the self-confidence one builds from accomplishing goals is the most beautiful thing in the world.*

MADONNA

And here speaks one who knows. Madonna has never just traded on her looks; she is an astute businesswoman who is always ready to change and move on when the time is right. She is constantly creating new goals and going for them. She recreates herself time and time again, and is always on to the next interesting thing. Of course we are fascinated by anyone who lives their life to the full in this way, particularly if they are in the public eye. Madonna, in her forties, demonstrates that she has more charisma, style and determination than most women half her age. She has accomplished this by always following her own path and by not being afraid to take chances and to be seen to be different. Her energy and fabulous figure are not the results of hours spent with a stylist but hours spent working on herself both physically and spiritually. Yes, of course she is talented and genetically blessed, but she has created her amazing ongoing success by constantly developing her gifts and making the most of herself, and this takes time, persistence and guts. Madonna will still be pulling in the crowds in 10 years time (if she decides that is what she wants to do).

You too can develop this confidence and strength of character. You build it by taking control of your life and creating and accomplishing your goals. The wonderful feeling of success puts you on top of the world. It is the ultimate high, and when you are exuding confidence you glow with life.

This is why confidence is top of the list of 'must haves' for every client I have ever worked with. At some point in our sessions the issue of self-confidence *always* emerges. Sometimes clients feel that a lack of confidence is at the root of all their problems, while for others it may affect only one area of their life. I want you to know that *everyone* has issues with lack of confidence; it's just that some people are better at hiding it than others. When I give a talk or workshop people often ask how it's possible to feel confident all the time, and I have to say that it's not! This is an important and helpful thing to know because it lets you off the hook and creates a more realistic approach to life. You can stop trying to be that perfectly composed and confident person who is full of self-assurance 24/7. Believe me, this person does not and *cannot* exist. We are only human! And being human means that we sometimes hold ourselves back when we could be moving forward. Doubts and self-critical thoughts can easily block our path if we let them. Let's face it, at times we all need to grasp our courage in both hands in order to do whatever it is that feels so daunting.

Cameron Diaz has an interesting view on this. She says: 'I don't think of anything as a "risk". I try every experience I can in life. When you are old, they say that your regrets aren't what you did but what you didn't do. So I like to take every opportunity I can.' Yes, opportunists always win the day and create new openings and possibilities for themselves (shrinking violets will never make a splash). I like to visualise an opportunity as an open door leading to a fresh and exciting new area of my life. Next time opportunity knocks and you are feeling nervous about stepping forward, try imagining this open door and seeing yourself going through, it smiling happily – this is a great strategy.

## Radiate confidence

You cannot live a life of no regrets unless you live to the full, and this means stepping forward, being noticed, grabbing chances and having a huge appetite for life. When you radiate confidence, you show the world that you believe in yourself and have the courage of your convictions. People pick up on this sort of vibrant, charismatic energy and will show respect and support for your ideas and opinions. You can see how this cycle all begins with you. Be sure of yourself, be true to yourself, go for what you want and you will have no regrets. Self-belief creates an all-win situation because there is never anything to lose. So you might go for it and fail but you took that chance, you made the choice to try, and that in itself can be enough to sustain your confidence. Confident people have a different attitude to life than do those who feel second-rate.

When you see or meet a confident person, remind yourself that they have *learned* to be like this. Negative people are inclined to believe that confidence is a gift that you receive at birth or don't (and that they didn't get it). Admittedly, there are those who have had a good start in life with a strong and supportive family, but even this cannot guarantee that magical quality of self-belief. There is only one way to become confident enough to believe in yourself and that is by recognising and changing all the negative beliefs that stand in your way *and you have to do this for yourself!* The smart approach is to

# QUICK TIP

YOUR BELIEFS ABOUT YOURSELF COME TRUE BECAUSE YOU ARE ALWAYS CREATING A SELF-FULFILLING PROPHECY. SO, FOR INSTANCE, IF YOU UNDERVALUE YOURSELF AND EXPECT TO FEEL INFERIOR, THEN YOU WILL. AND IF YOU APPRECIATE YOUR WORTH AND VALUE YOUR JUDGEMENT, THEN YOU WILL FEEL CONFIDENT.

THINK OF A SITUATION OR AREA OF YOUR LIFE IN WHICH YOU FEEL LOW IN CONFIDENCE. WHY DO YOU FEEL LIKE THIS? YOUR ANSWERS WILL DEMONSTRATE ALL SORTS OF 'EVIDENCE' THAT YOU HAVE COLLECTED TO 'PROVE' TO YOURSELF THAT YOU ARE NO GOOD, CAN'T DO ..., ALWAYS MESS UP, CAN'T TAKE RESPONSI-BILITY ... OR WHATEVER.

NOW CHALLENGE THIS VIEW. THINK OF TIMES WHEN YOU *HAVE* SHOWN THE QUALITIES THAT YOU THINK YOU LACK. COLLECT ALL THE EVIDENCE THAT YOU CAN TO CONTRADICT YOUR NEGATIVE SELF-BELIEFS AND *WRITE IT DOWN*.

ASK THE PEOPLE WHO LOVE YOU WHY THEY LOVE YOU. ASK YOUR CLOSE FRIENDS WHAT THEY SEE IN YOU. YOU WILL BE AMAZED BY WHAT YOU HEAR. YOU MAY HAVE STARTED TO TAKE YOUR PERSONAL STRENGTHS AND TALENTS FOR GRANTED. STOP DOING THIS! ADD THE POSITIVE OPINIONS OF OTHERS TO YOUR MOUNTING LIST OF EVIDENCE, WHICH WILL CONFIRM TO YOU THAT YOU ARE A PERSON OF WORTH AND ABILITY.

**CONFIDENT PEOPLE**

take this job extremely seriously and get on with it. The quicker you can let go of negative beliefs, the sooner you can feel the confidence you need to go for your goals. Get started on this immediately by recognising the voice of your inner critic.

## Your inner critic

You may often feel that if only a certain person didn't criticise you so much things would be easier for you, and for sure we all thrive on validation and positive feedback. But our most harmful attacker is never someone else; our most destructive critic is always ourselves. Just think of a time when someone criticised you and you knew their judgement was totally unfounded; at a time like this criticism is just like water off a duck's back and you can laugh it off. The disapproval of others only hits the mark if we believe, for even a moment, that what they are saying may be true.

Close your eyes for a few seconds and listen to the chatter that's going on in your head. All day, every day, hour in, hour out, asleep or awake, your mind keeps on doing its job: observing, thinking and making inner chit-chat. You are always talking to yourself, with all sorts of voices. One voice may be happy, supportive, and optimistic (for example: 'Keep going girl; you are doing really well') and another one can be undermining, blaming and critical (for example: 'You are useless. There you go again blowing it. When will you ever get it right?'). Psychologists refer to this fault-finding voice as the inner critic.

We all have this voice. It gives us messages such as, 'Whatever makes you feel that you deserve anything?', 'You are utterly useless', 'I hate you', 'You are so stupid/lazy /pathetic/worthless', 'You can never be confident', 'You're just a loser', 'You will never be good enough' ... This voice talks to you from your own personal selection of all the past criticisms you have heard and believed to be true. You may also notice that it speaks in a tone that you recognise from your child-hood. If you listen to and take notice of this voice you will always be low in confidence. And if you recognise that this voice has no power over you, you can step into a new super-confident cycle.

# Talking to yourself with confidence

- Start to listen out for your inner critic.

- Whenever you falter and doubt yourself, pause and try to remember your last thought. What was your inner critic saying to you?

- Ask yourself if your critical thoughts are really true. Pursue this and you will find that 99.9 per cent are untrue!

- Stop buying into critical beliefs that sap all your confidence.

- Choose to replace these criticisms with positive confidence-giving beliefs. For example:

| INNER CRITICISM | CONFIDENT BELIEF |
| --- | --- |
| I don't like myself. | I like myself. |
| I blame myself. | I accept myself. |
| I can't do that. | I can do this. |
| I am pathetic. | I am worth it. |
| I don't deserve anything. | I deserve the best. |

Keep working on this exercise. Rout out your inner critic and send it packing. As you let go of your belief in these criticisms, its voice will get quieter and quieter. Let a positive supportive voice shine though and you will become one of those confident people who have learned to believe in themselves.

# TIME OUT

THIS EXERCISE WILL RELAX YOUR EYES AND STIMULATE YOUR IMAGINATION AND INTUITION.

- SIT COMFORTABLY IN A CHAIR AND TAKE SOME SLOW DEEP BREATHS.

- SLOWLY LET YOUR CHIN DROP TOWARDS YOUR CHEST.

- DROP YOUR SHOULDERS AND RELAX THEM.

- REST YOUR HANDS ON YOUR THIGHS.

- CLOSE YOUR EYES AND LET YOUR INNER GAZE REST ON YOUR THIRD EYE (THIS IS THE SEAT OF YOUR INTUITION AND IS LOCATED BETWEEN YOUR EYEBROWS).

- BREATHE OUT AND LET GO OF YOUR GAZE.

- BREATHE IN AND ONCE AGAIN GAZE AT YOUR THIRD EYE.

- DO THIS SEVEN TIMES IN ALL.

BE SUPER-CONSCIOUS OF ANY INTUITIVE FEELINGS OR UNUSUAL AWARENESSES THAT YOU HAVE FOLLOWING THIS EXERCISE.

## The confidence to go for your dreams

I have always been fascinated by people who have the strength of character and the willpower to overcome seemingly incredible obstacles, which explains why I became glued to the reality TV programme *Operatunity*, which showed ordinary people being transformed into opera singers. Although, as a rule, I quickly lose interest in reality shows, this one got me hooked because one of the participants was a blind mother of three with a voice like an angel.

Denise Leigh hasn't had an easy life and has had to overcome many personal challenges to get to the point where she won joint first place on the show. The prize was the chance to sing the starring role of Gilda in Verdi's *Rigoletto* at the London Coliseum (home of the English National Opera), with the performance televised. What an inspiration Denise Leigh was: confident, brave and a real diva, despite all the practical difficulties that she faced. It took her 42 days to learn the score, only a few days less than it took Verdi to write it. And then there were all the problems of negotiating the stage and learning to move and respond like a sighted person. But none of this held her back. She had kept her ambition of singing at the Coliseum alive through years spent at home looking after her family, and when the opportunity knocked, she answered. Denise has all the qualities of a confident person. She is determined to do what she wants to do *in spite of all the obstacles*, and there were certainly many of those. Over the years she has remained powerfully determined, focused on her goal, dedicated to her musical talent, unafraid to take risks and patient in awaiting her moment.

So maybe your dreams aren't so far-fetched. Visualise them and bring them closer to reality. You can do whatever you have the confidence to do, and if you find yourself flagging and falling into negativity, just remember the sheer power of Denise Leigh, who worked and waited and believed in herself. This is the way to make your dreams come true.

# 25 tips to increase your confidence

1 Smile!

2 Always expect the best.

3 Say what you mean.

4 Network – get out there and get noticed.

5 Look for the silver lining.

6 Learn something new – stretch yourself in some way and see how flexible you can be.

7 Break an old habit that you have outgrown.

8 Keep your sense of humour.

9 Find time to meet up with your friends regularly.

10 Allocate yourself regular 'me' time, because you are worth it!

11 Stop moving goalposts and celebrate any and every step along the way.

12 Spend time with someone who is a positive influence on you.

13 Remember that everything changes and bad times will pass.

14 Keep at it; don't give up on yourself.

15 Don't blow things out of proportion – don't sweat the small stuff.

16 Buy a great pair of shoes and then plan a special occasion to wear them.

17 Take a step towards one of your goals.

18 Repeat this mantra: *I deserve the best.* You do of course!

19 Take some exercise – you will feel like a new woman. Move that body; even a short walk will do it.

20 Remember your strengths and demonstrate them.

21 Take that risk – you know you want to.

22 Don't put off the important things.

23 Stop comparing yourself with other people – you are an original.

24 Throw out those unfinished projects that weigh you down.

25 Believe that your dreams can come true and they will.

## Love your life

Confident people love life and they are brimming over with enthusiasm and positive expectation. This doesn't mean that they never have to face hard times or setbacks; it means that when they do, they can call on their reserves of optimism, trust and buoyancy to keep them afloat. Being able to love your life means that you can appreciate your downs as well as your ups. Sounds crazy? Well, not really; it's the sanest way to live. There are peaks and troughs in everyone's life, and the trick is to learn how to surf the waves of both extremes. Each time you face a challenge and ride it out, you will become stronger and more confident. Think of a time when you had to demonstrate your own powers of endurance, patience, tolerance or whatever in difficult circumstances. You came out of it feeling a greater sense of self-respect and self-worth, didn't you? But why wait for a bad patch to appreciate your gains? Confident people recognise that they are learning life's lessons all the time and that the sooner they learn from them, the quicker they will be able to move onward and upward in their life. This attitude only requires a subtle shift in awareness that creates an all-win situation out of every circumstance. If you can trust in the ultimate goodness of the universe, you will always be able to turn things around to serve you.

When I worked as a bereavement counsellor I met people

who were at their lowest ebb. The loss of a loved one is surely one of the greatest challenges we ever have to deal with, but the strength and courage of my clients was a privilege to witness. We all have the capacity to step into our own greatness, and the way to do this is easy. We simply need to learn to love and appreciate *all parts of our life*. Everything happens for a purpose, even if it's hard to see at the time. Confident people maintain their belief in the benevolence of the universe *even when the going is rough*. Think of your life as a training course. Every day you are studying the curriculum (life's lessons). Instead of ranting and raving at the unfairness and complications that confront you, why not take a philosophical approach? Look for the hidden meaning in all things; search for the lesson you are being taught, learn it and then move on. As you build your stores of confidence you are creating reserves to fall back on when you are in need. Get confident about the process of life and recognise that there is significance and purpose in everything that happens to you. Love your life and your life will give you back that magical quality we call confidence.

## Project a positive self-image

What sort of person do you think you are? If I asked you to choose your top 10 adjectives to describe yourself what would they be? Write them down and see what you come up with. Are you creative, friendly, kind, tolerant, skilful, talented, sensitive, articulate and intelligent? Are you boring, lazy, fearful, troubled, shy, controlling, critical, miserable, passive and untalented? Your list is probably a mixture of negative and positive characteristics. The words you use to describe yourself create your self-image – the impression you present to the rest

# QUICK TIP

DUCKS SWIM IN WATER BUT THEY NEVER GET WET, HENCE THE SAYING 'LIKE WATER OFF A DUCK'S BACK'. THE DUCK LIVES IN THE WATER BUT ISN'T AFFECTED BY IT. THIS IS THE WAY YOU NEED TO LEARN TO LIVE YOUR LIFE. YOUR RESERVES OF CONFIDENCE GET LOWER WHEN YOU ALLOW YOURSELF TO BECOME TOO AFFECTED AND DISTRACTED BY ALL THAT IS HAPPENING AROUND YOU.

- THE NEXT TIME YOU FEEL EMOTIONALLY STRETCHED, ASK YOURSELF THIS QUESTION: 'WHY AM I LETTING THIS GET TO ME?'

- NOW IMAGINE THAT DUCK SWIMMING IN THE POND AND THE WATER DROPLETS ROLLING OFF ITS WATER-PROOFED FEATHERS. YOU CAN BE JUST AS UNPERTURBED BY THE STRONG FORCES IN YOUR LIFE.

- VISUALISE THE DUCK AND SAY TO YOURSELF, 'THIS IS JUST LIKE WATER OFF A DUCK'S BACK TO ME.'

CULTIVATE AN IMAGE OF YOURSELF AS A PERSON WHO CAN EASILY LET THINGS GO. YOU DON'T SWEAT THE SMALL STUFF AND YOU DON'T LET THINGS GET TO YOU. YOU ROLL WITH THE PUNCHES AND HAVE THE SELF-CONFIDENCE TO KNOW THAT NOTHING AND NO ONE HAS THE POWER TO DISTURB YOUR LIFE.

AFTER YOU HAVE DONE THIS EXERCISE A FEW TIMES, THE IMAGE OF THE DUCK WILL BE ENOUGH TO GET YOU BACK ON COURSE (WITH A SMILE ON YOUR FACE).

of the world. Are you creating the right impression? If your self-image is positive and assertive, others will see and feel your confidence and will show you the respect you deserve. But if your self-image is negative, you will come over as a person who is lacking in confidence and unsure of yourself, and unfortunately this will affect the way that others treat you.

If your list contains any negative characteristics, delete them. Create a list of positive qualities and start to project them into your life: live them and become them! Change your self-image by changing yourself. Take any negatives on your list and act as if the opposite were true. For example if you think you are boring, act as if you are fascinating. Get out there and fake it until you make it! And make it you will, because as you project your new image so you will become it. Don't ever believe the least of yourself; you are so much more than you think you are. Every time you belittle yourself you are letting yourself down and reinforcing your negative self-beliefs. So become the best of yourself and show the world what you are really made of. Believe me, you will be glad you did when the newly confident you starts to attract increasing amounts of positive and vibrant energy (fresh breaks, connections with interesting and creative people, a new appetite for life). What are you waiting for? Throw out those images that don't work for you. Yes, you can do this because (don't forget) you created them in the first place. Inside every insecure and uncertain person is a confident and self-assured individual who is *dying* to get out! Create a positive self-image and *let her out!*

# TIME OUT

## FIVE-MINUTE RELAXATION

Relax and get totally comfortable.

- Think of a time when you let yourself down in some way. What aspects of your negative self-image were you operating from. Don't go down a self-critical path here; just remain detached and think realistically.

- Still with this air of detachment, think of ways in which you could have supported yourself in this situation. What positive qualities would you have needed to project?

- Now close your eyes and allow your breathing to slow down. When you are feeling physically and mentally relaxed, create the following visualisation.

  Imagine that you have all the positive characteristics that you need to be true to yourself in any situation you might meet. Take these qualities one at a time and 'see' yourself projecting them out into the world. Feel what it would be like to be confident, assertive, capable, intelligent, creative, etc.

- Return to your original situation and *see* and *feel* the positive elements of your self-image which would have allowed you to be true to

YOURSELF IN THE CIRCUMSTANCES. GET RIGHT INTO
THE SKIN OF THESE POSITIVE ELEMENTS AND KNOW
EXACTLY HOW IT FEELS TO DEAL CONFIDENTLY AND
CREATIVELY WITH THIS SITUATION.

- WHEN YOU ARE READY, OPEN YOUR EYES AND COME
BACK INTO THE ROOM.

NOW YOU KNOW HOW TO SIMULATE THE EXACT
FEELINGS THAT GO WITH YOUR POSITIVE SELF-IMAGE,
AND YOU CAN EASILY PROJECT THEM INTO REAL-LIFE
SCENARIOS. YOU CAN 'ACT AS IF' AND TURN THINGS
AROUND FOR YOURSELF. THE NEXT TIME YOU ARE FACED
WITH A SIMILAR SITUATION, YOU WILL KNOW THAT YOU
DON'T HAVE TO LET YOURSELF DOWN; YOU CAN DEMON-
STRATE ALL THE CONFIDENCE YOU NEED.

# Look Good and Feel Great

*I don't believe makeup and the right hairstyle alone can make a woman beautiful. The most radiant woman in the room is the one full of life and experience.*

SHARON STONE

I know you probably wish your legs were longer, your bum was smaller, your eyes were bigger, your nose was straighter ... But let's start this chapter on a high note! You are feeling positive, motivated and focused and do not intend to play the victim in any area of your life, and this includes the looks department! I have never met any woman who is totally satisfied with the way she looks, so accept that this is the norm in our society and get on and make the very best of what you have.

Celebrity glitz and glamour have an insidious way of undermining our own self-image. Even though we know that those photographs of gorgeous young models have been airbrushed to perfection, we can *still* find ourselves making unfavourable comparisons with the reflection we see in the mirror. Movie stars and celebrities have stylists, hairdressers, dressers and the rest hovering around them each time they make a public appearance, so it's not surprising that they are looking their best. And when they lose their youthful good looks the press is on their backs, as if it's a crime to get older and show your age. A popular tabloid featured a terrible picture of Melanie Griffiths showing 'the true cost of Melanie's battle to stay young'. Over-use of Botox and the appearance of crows' feet (inevitable in anyone who is over 40) made Melanie look her age. We can only feel sorry for the actress who is so depressed by her looks that she says of her younger husband Antonio Banderas: 'He knows what I've become – old and ugly.'

And have you noticed how many high-profile women lose large amounts of weight when they hit the big time? Remember the Spice Girls and their message of Girl Power? When Mel C joined the band she says, 'I was pretty normal – I was a dancer, so I was conscious of my body, but I'd never had an eating problem.' Then one of the financial backers of the band said to her, 'You'll never do a back flip with thighs that big.' And for Mel that was it; she knew she was going to be on TV, and she knew that TV makes people look fatter than they are. She stopped eating properly and began a punishing exercise regime. She says, 'My overriding memory is that I was always hungry.' She is now happy to be a normal weight. In all, three of the five Spice Girls have revealed that they have had eating disorders – not so much a case of Girl Power then; more an example of loss of power.

Atomic Kitten star Natasha Hamilton recently outraged parents of her young fans. When asked how she got back into shape so quickly after the birth of her baby son, Natasha smiled at the photographers surrounding her and said, 'That's easy. I just don't eat. That's how I've done it – the way to a nice backside is not to eat.' So Natasha (voted Rear of the Year) may be looking good but she probably isn't feeling so great.

# You're only as attractive as you feel

When did you feel at your most beautiful? Yes, it might have been that time when your hair looked great and your designer outfit was just right for the occasion; looking good can certainly give us a great boost of confidence and wellbeing. But let's not forget the times when you felt fabulous *even though* it was a bad hair day. When you remember these occasions, you remind yourself of something vitally important: you are only ever as attractive as you feel inside. My greatest feeling-fabulous moments include the three times when I had just given birth, certainly very low in the glamour stakes but extremely high on excitement and love. And I can come away from the gym, with the buzz of those feelgood endorphins rushing around my body, feeling great even though I'm hot and sweaty and my hair is sticking up all over the place.

The truth is that we always want to *feel* our best, and while this may also include looking good, *it doesn't depend on it*. If you are glowing with health and vitality, then you feel amazing and look amazing because your aura will be charged with positive energy and you will look and feel full of life.

# The Bridget Jones syndrome

A major survey has revealed that most of us are suffering from this unfortunate syndrome. The symptoms include lack of body confidence and a total preoccupation with our looks. Ninety per cent of the 5,000 women who took part in the survey said that they were 'depressed' by the appearance of their body, and one in ten admitted to being on a 'constant' diet.

Does this mean we are shallow and fixated by superficiality? Are we over-obsessed with our wobbly bits and pieces? I don't think so. Let's be realistic here, we do want to reach for our best in *every* area of our life, and why shouldn't we? We want to love our lives; live meaningfully; go for our goals and look pretty damn good while we're doing it! So, as in all things, we need to find a balanced approach to getting all that we want. You know the techniques for being a go-getter rather than a victim; you can use these very same strategies to stop yourself being victimised and enslaved by unreasonable and impossible self-expectations. For example, if you spend your time comparing yourself with youthful, leggy models, you are always going to be unhappy. Similarly, if you are small and you long to be tall, or you are long-limbed and you want to be petite, you are *wasting your yearnings*. Recognise what you can alter and what you can't, make peace with the impossible and get going on what you can change. Take stock and let your desires be for something that you can achieve. Remember how desire is such a great motivator? Get real and use it wisely. Oh, and referring back to those things that you can't change, decide to make the most of them. They are what make you original, unusual and special, so why not make a feature of them?

---

## QUICK TIP

MODERN MAKEUP TECHNIQUES AND FABULOUS NEW PRODUCTS MAKE IT POSSIBLE FOR US TO MINIMISE AND MAXIMISE MANY ASPECTS OF OUR APPEARANCE. IF YOU THINK YOUR EYES ARE TOO CLOSE TOGETHER, YOUR LIPS TOO THIN, YOUR SKIN TOO BLOTCHY ...

• TAKE YOURSELF OFF FOR A PROFESSIONAL MAKEOVER (AT THE MAKEUP COUNTER IN MOST GOOD DEPART-MENT STORES) AND LEARN THE TRICKS YOU NEED TO

---

KNOW TO DISGUISE THE BITS YOU WANT TO HIDE AND MAKE THE MOST OF YOUR ASSETS. TAKE THE TIME TO FIND OUT HOW YOU CAN LOOK YOUR BEST AND WHICH PRODUCTS SUIT YOU.

• SPEND MONEY ON HAVING YOUR HAIR CUT BY A REALLY GOOD STYLIST. WATCH THE BLOW-DRYING TECHNIQUE SO THAT YOU CAN DO IT AT HOME. ASK FOR ADVICE ON WHICH HAIR PRODUCTS ARE BEST FOR YOU.

• PERHAPS BLACK ISN'T YOUR BEST COLOUR AFTER ALL! IF YOU WANT TO KNOW WHAT SUITS YOU, THERE ARE PLENTY OF EXPERTS AROUND. IMAGE SPECIALISTS AND COLOUR CONSULTANTS CAN OPEN NEW POSSIBILITIES FOR YOU. TRY THEM IF YOU NEED A CHANGE.

• DEVELOP A LOOK AND A STYLE THAT SUITS YOU. DON'T BUY CLOTHES JUST BECAUSE THEY ARE FASHIONABLE OR BECAUSE THEY LOOK GOOD ON SOMEONE ELSE. CULTIVATE YOUR OWN INDIVIDUAL IMAGE AND YOU WILL BECOME KNOWN FOR YOUR INDIVIDUALITY AND SENSE OF PERSONAL FLAIR.

• BY ALL MEANS ENJOY THE GLOSSY HYPE OF MAGAZINES, BUT BEAR IN MIND THAT IT IS A GLORIOUS FANTASY WORLD OF GLAMOUR. DON'T TAKE THE GLITZ TOO SERIOUSLY AND THEN YOU WILL BE FREE TO ENJOY BUYING NEW CLOTHES AND MAKEUP WITHOUT FEELING INTIMIDATED IN ANY WAY.

• HAVE FUN WITH NEW PRODUCTS AND FASHION AND TRY REINVENTING YOURSELF. YOUR LOOK IS ANY LOOK THAT YOU LOVE, SO GET ADVENTUROUS WHENEVER YOU FEEL LIKE A CHANGE.

# Looking after yourself

You don't need me to tell you that to appear and feel at the top of your game you need to look after yourself. Everywhere you look in magazines, in the papers, on television, you will find advice on how to make the very best of yourself. You know all you need to know about eating sensibly, drinking lots of water, taking enough exercise and getting plenty of sleep. The crucial point is *are you doing these things?*

It's often harder to do what we know is good for us when we are feeling a bit down. Even though we know that a walk or a trip to the gym would cheer us up (raise endorphin levels and increase our body confidence and sense of self-respect) we may be more likely to curl up on the sofa with a glass of wine. And if that's how you feel, then go with it. There is nothing to be gained by listening to your inner critic at times like these (saying for example 'You are such a slob. Think of the calories in that wine. Why can't you get off your lazy butt...'). When it's all too much, just sit it out until your mood lifts a little and your motivation returns. I know only too well how easy it is for clients to beat themselves up when it comes to their fitness regime, and I always advise a more relaxed approach. You can never force yourself against your will to keep to a routine (however healthy and good it may be for you); only your motivation and focus will keep you on target.

Anna Wintour, Editor of US *Vogue*, is a purposeful and determined woman who is at the top of her career ladder. A TV programme about her showed her usual start to the day: 6.30am get up; 7am play tennis; 8am have hair and makeup done professionally; 9am leave for the office in a chauffeur-driven car; 9.30am arrive in the office looking impeccably gorgeous! And (one expects) feeling on top form. So there you go, girls – a sure-fire template for looking good and feeling great. Yes, she can afford all this attention, but hats off to Anna, what focus and drive! Would you be prepared to go through that routine every morning of the week (even if you could afford to)?

## Successful weight control

The slimming business is huge, and with diet books and exercise videos galore, none of us can be in doubt of the basic facts: to maintain a healthy weight we need adequate exercise and a sensible, balanced diet. I'm sure you know all the 'right' and 'wrong' things to do in order to be slim, and you will probably have tried some of the countless diets around. But in spite of all the available information you are one of the majority if you are still struggling to reach your desired weight.

---

### TIME OUT

GO AND LOOK IN THE MIRROR. NOTICE YOUR REACTIONS – THE THOUGHTS AND FEELINGS YOU HAVE.

LOOK DEEPLY INTO YOUR OWN EYES AND SAY, 'I LOVE YOU.' SAY IT AGAIN. SPEND A FEW MOMENTS LOOKING AT YOUR WHOLE BODY AND APPRECIATING ALL THAT IT DOES FOR YOU. LOVE YOUR HANDS (AREN'T THEY AMAZING?); LOVE YOUR EYES; LOVE YOUR EARS, YOUR NOSE ... APPRECIATE THIS FABULOUS AND MIRACULOUS MACHINE THAT CARRIES YOU ABOUT. LOOK BEYOND THE IMAGE YOU SEE AND RECOGNISE YOUR PHYSICAL PERFECTION.

---

A staggering 95 per cent of dieters fail to achieve permanent weight loss (according to a survey by *Psychology Today*). We need to go beyond calorie counting and special recipes if we want to find out why.

When your inner resolve starts to flag, it's only too easy to reach for the biscuit tin (or for whatever takes your fancy) and throw all caution to the winds. Motivation and willpower are the keys to successful weight control. Sports psychologists tell us that winning has as much to do with mental stamina as it has with ability. To be successful at anything you need to sustain a positive and upbeat approach so that you can stay focused on your goals, maintain your commitment, keep your sense of humour, overcome any setbacks and remain flexible in your approach. You can achieve anything once you believe that you can, so trust your own commitment to your weight control goals and begin!

## Your personal weight control plan

This simple 6-point plan uses techniques that you will recognise from Part 1 of this book. You might like to buy a separate notebook to use as your weight control journal.

### 1 State your goals

Once you have specified your goals and *written them down*, you have taken the most important step towards achieving them. The most powerful statements of intent are well defined and precise (indecisive thinking leads to muddled action). Take some time here to really think about what you want to achieve. Do you want to lose a specific amount of weight? Are you trying to maintain your present weight? Do you want to change your eating habits? Would you like to drop a dress size?

Do you want to tone up and feel fitter? Add anything else that you can think of.

Write your goals in your journal and be realistic about your time frame. Break down your goals into bite-sized pieces. Remember that you can only create success by taking one step at a time. Don't set yourself targets that you cannot meet. Have you ever done this and so sabotaged your weight control plan? If so, reflect on this and learn from it. Know that if you create unrealistic goals (too much too soon) you will fail. So make some short-term goals (easily attainable) and the fulfilment of these will motivate and encourage you.

Make a statement of intent of your longer-term goals. Write each goal in your statement at the top of a separate page in your notebook, for example 'I want to eat a healthier diet,' 'I want to lose X pounds,' 'I want to go down one dress size,' 'I want to feel more in control of my eating habits.'

Now think about how you can achieve each of these goals. What is the first small step you must take? Be clear about the steps you will be taking to fulfil each goal: the food you will eat, the exercise you will take, the weight you intend to lose ... Write your daily and/or weekly plans under each long-term goal. From these you can create your short-term targets.

As you break down your goals they will begin to look more manageable. You will start to think, 'Yes, I can do this' – and it's true, you can! Think of your short-term goals as daily achievable targets (which they are). Each day builds on the strength of what has gone before. As you become more confident about your inner strength and determination, your weight control plan will get easier and easier.

## 2  Maintain a positive focus

Keep focusing on your targets and these goals will become more and more accessible. Bring the new you into your life right now by using positive statements about yourself. Repeat any of the following affirmations to help keep you on track.

- I am looking good and feeling good.
- Every day I become more resolved to achieve my goals.
- My diet is healthy and is doing me good.
- I can easily achieve my targets.
- I love exercising; it makes me feel great.
- I deserve to look and feel my very best.

Don't worry if you find it hard to believe these statements. Remember that they work by first contradicting and then by replacing any of your limiting negative beliefs. So keep on saying them and they will eventually become true for you. Create your own affirmations if you wish, but make sure they are always positive and that they are always in the present tense. If you affirm that you *will become* slim and healthy then the realisation of your goal will always stay in the future. Say, sing, think, these affirmations any time you can (in the car, in the bath, out shopping ... anywhere). The more you repeat them the quicker they will work. Write them down and make a note of any emotions they arouse in you. Pin up your affirmations around your home and put them on your desk and in your handbag to keep reminding yourself of your goals and your determination to realise them. Bring your new positive thoughts into the very centre of your life and just watch them come true!

## 3  See yourself at your best

Just as positive thoughts help you to create and reach new goals, so do the mental images that you carry in your head. What you continually 'see' in your mind's eye has an uncanny way of becoming true in some way. So how do you see yourself? Step out of any old negative self-images right now! Imagine the new you: vibrant, radiant, at your ideal weight, toned, fit and happy with yourself. It is a psychological fact that we become what we think we are, so start creating some positive mental pictures of how you look and feel. Encourage yourself in any way you find helpful. For example, if you have a photo of your slim self, why not place it in a prominent position to remind you that you can be like this again. Or focus your attention on an item of clothing that you are aiming to fit into. Do whatever you can to make your new mental self-image enter your life in a realistic way, and before you know it you really will be looking your best!

## 4  Visualise your goals

This fabulous technique takes the previous step into a different dimension and has stunning effects. While surrounding yourself with positive images will encourage you and remind you of your targets and goals, visualisation actually helps to *imprint* them firmly in your mind.

Choose a time when you can have a few minutes of peace and quiet. Sit comfortably and close your eyes. Relax and then concentrate on creating an action movie in your head. Visualise yourself going for your goals and being successful. In your mind's eye 'see' yourself looking and feeling great. Make the pictures as vivid and bold as possible. See your new self and feel the emotions that will come with the realisation of your goals. Let your pictures move and include the other people in your life. Be creative and go where the feelings take you. For example you may see and hear others telling you how good you look. Keep your pictures positive, supportive and realistic. Now you can recreate those pictures in a flash, whenever you have a moment to spare. Keep practising this technique because it will reinforce all the other steps that you are taking.

## 5 Be your own best friend

You are the only person who can make your dreams come true, so become your own best friend. Support and encourage yourself all the way. Begin to observe the ways that you talk to yourself. Stop using self-criticisms and replace them with encouraging and upbeat commentary. For example you might talk to yourself about how you are achieving your goals and how well you are doing. A friendly 'you can do it' statement can work wonders for your resolution and willpower.

## 6 Go for it!

Bring together all your techniques in a short routine that you can repeat at intervals throughout the day. Choose some positive affirmations and visualisations that suit your needs. Make sure you keep your inner talk confident and persuasive. Surround yourself with positive reminders (photos, healthy food, written affirmations, etc.) to keep you focused. Let yourself off the hook: if you fall by the wayside, just pick yourself up and carry on where you left off (don't use a fall from grace as an excuse to stop your weight control pro-gramme).

And before you begin, you might want to consider the pros and cons of telling other people what you are doing. If you feel that this will help keep you motivated, then by all means do it, but make sure that you choose to tell only those who will positively support you.

I hope that your new insights will help you to maintain your resolve and to feel a new sense of confidence in yourself. Always remember that self-criticisms lead into negativity, so keep those positive affirmations going. Allow yourself to bend the rules occasionally and then let yourself off immediately – this will prevent that natural inclination to feel deprived and then to compensate by over-eating. When you combine good eating habits with a positive outlook, you will find that you really *can* reach your ideal weight and *stay there*!

## Body confidence

However successful your weight control plan, however great your exercise regime, it is possible that you still may not be satisfied with the way you look and feel about yourself. If you are trying to be something that you cannot be, then you will never achieve your goals. It is important to recognise that women (and increasingly men) are feeling more and more pressurised to look a certain way – the way that fashion dictates.

Your weight *does not* dictate your level of body confidence. Losing weight and toning your body may not be all it takes to give you a positive self-image. Much of your appearance is genetically determined and there are some physical things that you just cannot change, so be realistic. And be warned: if you are chasing a 'perfect' face or body, you will never be happy and you will never be confident about the way you look.

# Your body confidence test*

Answer 'yes', 'no' or 'sometimes' to the following questions to find out how you really feel about your body.

1 Do you feel physically strong and powerful?

2 Do you hate any part of your body?

3 Would you say that you are obsessed by the food you eat/don't eat?

4 Do you feel free to enjoy eating?

5 Do you weigh yourself more than twice a week?

6 Do you think you would be happier if you lost weight?

7 Are you ever embarrassed by your body?

8 Do you compare yourself with other women?

9 Do you think looks are more important than personal qualities and abilities?

10 Would you like to have a positive self-image?

*Adapted from my book, *Be Yourself.*

---

I think our tendency to criticise our own appearance is an extension of the belief that we are not 'good enough' just the way we are. Ask people you know how they feel about their looks. You will be amazed to hear your skinny friend complaining about her fat thighs and your beautiful colleague moaning about her nose, hair ... whatever. So take heart, you are not the only one who falls into the trap of undermining your looks by measuring yourself against unrealistic and impossible standards. When you next start worrying about how you look, get out of this negative loop immediately. Stop criticising yourself and choose instead to concentrate on your physical assets. Express your originality and style and don't ever take the fashion game too seriously. Make peace with your appearance and work on your positive feelings about yourself. Love your looks, and your inner confidence will give you the radiance of a truly beautiful woman.

## 10 tips for looking good and feeling great

1 Love and appreciate all your physical features.
2 Walk tall and carry yourself with pride.
3 Smile, smile, smile – you will look and feel confident.
4 Forget about your appearance and concentrate on other people.
5 Get enthusiastic and interested and you will look and feel fully alive.
6 Never compare yourself with anybody else. Be a first-rate version of yourself.
7 Look beyond the image; you are only as attractive as you feel!
8 Optimise your best features and make peace with the rest.
9 Eat well and exercise.
10 Enjoy life and remember that it is your *inner qualities* that make you the amazing woman that you are.

# TIME OUT

## FIVE-MINUTE RELAXATION

TAKE FIVE MINUTES TO REALLY APPRECIATE YOUR BODY.

- SIT OR LIE DOWN, CLOSE YOUR EYES AND BREATHE SLOWLY AND DEEPLY. FEEL THE WEIGHT OF YOUR BODY.

- TURN YOUR ATTENTION TO YOUR SKELETON. BECOME AWARE OF ALL THE BONES IN YOUR BODY. APPRECIATE ALL THAT YOUR BONES DO FOR YOU.

- THINK OF ALL YOUR INTERNAL ORGANS AND ALL THE WORK THEY DO TO KEEP YOU ALIVE. APPRECIATE THEIR AMAZINGNESS.

- BECOME AWARE OF YOUR SENSES AND HOW MUCH YOU VALUE THEM.

- BE GLAD AND GIVE THANKS TO THIS MIRACULOUS MACHINE THAT IS YOUR BODY. YOU WOULD NOT BE HERE WITHOUT IT.

- BE GRATEFUL FOR YOUR LIFE.

- WHEN YOU ARE READY, GRADUALLY OPEN YOUR EYES AND SLOWLY BRING YOURSELF BACK TO NORMAL CONSCIOUSNESS.

# Be Happy

*For a long time it had seemed to me
that life was about to begin – real life.
But there was always some obstacle in
the way, something to be got through
first, some unfinished business, time still
to be served, a debt to be paid. Then life
would begin. At last it dawned on me
that these obstacles were my life.*

ALFRED D'SOUZA

Are you waiting for your real life to begin? If so, when will you know that it has started? And what exactly has to happen before you can really get going and have a good time? I often hear clients say they know that once they have achieved this, that or the other they will be happy. But consider this: what if happiness isn't an ideal state that we are working towards but rather a state of mind that we can create even if we don't get to reach all our goals this week? Cut yourself some slack, give yourself a break and recognise that happiness is available to you right here and now (yes, even if you are not in the perfect relationship, *still* haven't got below 10 stone, can't afford a bigger flat ...). It's true: you can be happy whenever you choose to be, there really are no external conditions involved. And if you don't believe me (you *know* that you will be happy forever once you meet the man of your dreams) then just keep an open mind while you read this chapter.

Tony Blair's cleverest advisors, at the Downing Street strategy unit, have studied the issue of whether we are experiencing enough joy in our lives, and the sad conclusion of their report was that we are not. These politicians and economists are puzzled and fascinated by the fact that higher standards of living have not made us any happier than we used to be. Their report states that, 'Despite large increases in national income and expenditure over the past 30 years, levels of satisfaction have not increased commensurately.' James Wilsdon, head strategist of the think tank Demos, predicts a future in which government preoccupations may have to change in order to reflect the things that really make us happy. He says: 'It would mean the government shifting the focus to friendship rather than fast cars, community rather than Caribbean holidays, the environment rather than the endless accumulation of material goods.'

Yes, we all want more money, of course we do, but the experts agree that in fact, unless you are in the bottom third of the economic pile, the extent of your wealth will have *no bearing on the state of your happiness*. How many more clothes, DVD players, computers, cars, televisions ... do you need? Does retail therapy always work and how lasting are its results? I'm sure you are familiar with the buzz that comes from a *serious* shopping session. Buying things makes us feel good. But you also know that whatever you bring home in those bags can never bring you lasting happiness and fulfilment.

# So who wants money, sex, power and status?

Well, most of us actually. It has been said that our culture is fixated on how to get more of these four things. Yes, we all want enough money to live on, and sex, power and status can be pretty cool, but the fact remains that these things alone cannot ever bring us long-term contentment – and sometimes they may even get in the way of our happiness.

The think tank's revelations support the wisdom recognised in many ancient spiritual and mystical traditions that *happiness does not come from getting what you want but rather from wanting what you have*. So enjoy the goodies of the material world but understand that happiness is a state of mind. It lies within you and not outside you in any shape or form. This is brilliant news and means you can stop feeling miserable immediately! You are no longer dependent on what happens to you or who happens to enter your life (or doesn't) or whether you can afford those divine Jimmy Choo strappy sandals. You can *choose* to feel happy or not. It's as simple as that.

# Get your happiness hormones flowing

Hypnotist Paul McKenna has been studying optimum states, happiness and peak experiences for many years, and he has concluded that we can train our mind to be happy! Of course, if you are suffering from clinical depression you will need medical help, but the majority of us really can help ourselves to happiness.

Paul says: 'Happiness is not something you can buy or earn – it's a state of mind and body. It is the response to what is happening in your life, and the good news is that you can learn to experience that response much more often.' Think about happiness and how it feels for you. Remember a time when you were very happy and try to recollect the exact feelings. Did you feel light-hearted? Did you experience a deep sense of peace? How did your body react? Get into the feelings as much as you can. This is the response state that Paul is talking about.

You probably know about the natural feel-good hormones produced by the body. These are called endorphins and we release them when we laugh, do physical exercise, relax and make love – which is why these activities are so good for you! Paul has developed a simple exercise that taps into our ability to release endorphins at will. He suggests that you visualise an 'endorphin button' in your mind. It could have 'endorphins' written on it or a smiley face or any symbol you like. See it now. Imagine pressing this button and experiencing the happiness response we talked about earlier. Imagine pressing it twice and getting double the happiness input. Play around with this technique. It may take a while to get the hang of it, but if you practise pressing the button and feeling your response enough times you will be able to release endorphins at will. What a brilliant practical tip!

## Happiness is ...

- **Staying in the moment.** When you can bring your full attention to the present moment you will feel happy. Try this exercise. Think about your anxieties – all those things that are stopping you from feeling happy right now. You will find that they are all about the future (what may or may not happen) or about the past (regrets, guilt, recriminations, lack of forgiveness, etc.). Why do you burden yourself so unnecessarily? The only time we ever really have is NOW!

# TIME OUT

Why not try releasing some of those lovely endorphins by relaxing with this time out?

In his wonderful book *Peace is Every Step*, the famous Zen master and peace activist Thich Nhat Hanh tells a simple story about the Buddha and a flower.

One day the Buddha held up a flower to an audience of 1,250 nuns and monks. Everyone was silent, thinking and trying to comprehend the hidden meaning of this gesture. Then eventually a monk called Mahakashyapa smiled at the Buddha and the flower. The Buddha smiled back at him and said, 'I have a treasure of insight, and I have transmitted it to Mahakashyapa.'

Thich Nhat Hanh says that this story has been discussed by many generations of Zen students and that Buddhists continue to look for its meaning. He says, 'To me the meaning is quite simple. When someone holds up a flower and shows it to you he wants you to see it. If you keep thinking, you miss the flower. The person who was not thinking, who was just himself, was able to encounter the flower in depth, and he smiled.'

Try being completely aware in this present moment. Stop thinking about the future and the past and just *be* in this moment. Unwind, breathe deeply and enjoy it to the full. Be yourself, relax, smile and see how happy this makes you feel.

Sometimes when clients get over-involved in the past or worry about the future I ask them to stop and tell me where they are. Where is the place where that action happened? Where is the place they are so worried about ending up? And the answer of course is *nowhere!* There is no past or future. The past has gone and the future is yet to come; only the present moment is real! If you load the future with negative concerns, this is what you will draw into your life. The beliefs, thoughts and visualisations that you are having in the present are creating your future NOW! So be mindful of this moment, live it and love it and you will both feel happy *and* create a happy future.

- **Living life to the full.** When you say or feel that you 'have to' do something it takes all the joy out of the prospect doesn't it? But when you become a person who *wants* to do it, something magical happens in your life. In a recent interview, Oscar-winning actress Hilary Swank said she has learned that she can do anything as long as she sets her mind to it. I was struck by her next comment: 'I don't do anything halfway.' You will never, ever be happy if you do things halfway. When I was growing up my father used to say, 'If a thing is worth doing, it's worth doing properly.' I didn't always appreciate his wisdom then, but now I do, *and he is still saying it to me* Thanks, Dad. It's good to be reminded.

  What both Hilary and my dad are saying is: live life to the full! Why would we choose not to do this? Where is the joy in a half-hearted gesture? If you are doing *anything* halfway, ask yourself why. You might find that you are doing it to please someone else. If so, perhaps it's time to stop. There is no doubt that if you are living half-heartedly you will always be unhappy. Choose to become an enthusiastic and wholehearted 'want to' person, and if you really can't drop your 'have tos', *fake* some enthusiasm until you can feel it.

- **Being able to let go.** What are you hanging on to that causes you unhappiness? Your immediate answer might be 'nothing', but just think again. Many of my clients discover that their biggest obstacles to progress and change are actually to be found *inside themselves*: in their own attitude to their past and their lack of forgiveness for themselves and for others. I often ask clients to create a Because List. Here are a few examples of the kinds of issues they identify:

*Because my mother never praised me
I can never feel confident.*

*Because he left me I can never trust
another man.*

*Because I did something wrong I deserve
to be punished for the rest of my life.*

*Because they told me I was stupid at school
I feel that I can't train for a new career.*

Are you blaming yourself or anyone else for your present situation? Write your own Because List and see what comes up. Hanging on to the past will stop you moving forward; let go and forgive whoever needs to be forgiven and you will feel a new lightness of heart and spirit. You can let go of anything that doesn't work for you any more: negative beliefs, victim behaviour (being a doormat), rescuing behaviour (being a saviour), unequal relationships (being a bully or being bullied), sadness, pessimism, hatred of another person, self-dislike ... What would you like to let go of? Decide to drop it and move forward. Nothing ever holds you back except yourself!

Happiness comes to you when you feel free to be yourself and can live your life to the full. Let go of anything that holds you back. Reach for your dreams, appreciate your wonderful life and be glad to be alive.

## The Glad Game

You may have seen the recent TV adaptation of *Pollyanna*, starring Amanda Burton as Pollyanna's embittered Aunt Polly. The original story, written by Eleanor Hodgman Porter, was published in 1913 and became a runaway word-of-mouth success, eventually selling over one million copies. Pollyanna Whittier is the daughter of a penniless missionary who preaches the sermon of gladness. The Reverend Whittier has discovered that there are *800* instances in the Bible where God instructs his children to be glad and rejoice, and from this he concludes that He must have wanted us to live in happiness.

One Christmas, Pollyanna has asked for a china doll. But when the holiday hamper arrives from the Missionary Ladies Aid Society there has been some mistake and it contains a pair of crutches for Pollyanna instead of the doll. She is so down-hearted and miserable that her father devises a game to see if they can think of one good thing about getting crutches as a Christmas present. Of course you can guess what they come up with: Pollyanna doesn't need them! And so the Glad Game was created.

# QUICK TIP

YOU WILL ATTRACT WHATEVER YOU THINK ABOUT AND FOCUS UPON. IF YOU PRIORITISE HAPPINESS, THIS IS WHAT YOU WILL GET. MAKE HAPPINESS YOUR NUMBER ONE GOAL FOR A DAY AND SEE WHAT HAPPENS.

- WAKE UP AND APPRECIATE YOUR LIFE.

- SING IN THE SHOWER AND LIFT YOUR SPIRITS.

- SMILE AND FEEL THAT ENDORPHIN LIFT.

- TAKE A LIGHTER NOTE WHENEVER THE ATMOSPHERE GETS HEAVY.

- NOTICE HOW OTHERS RESPOND TO YOUR LIGHT-HEARTED MOOD.

- DON'T USE ANY CRITICAL WORDS WHEN YOU SPEAK OF OTHER PEOPLE.

- SUSPEND YOUR JUDGEMENTS.

- LOOK FOR THE BEST IN EVERY SITUATION.

- STAY IN THE MOMENT AND DON'T DRIFT INTO WORRIES ABOUT THE PAST OR FUTURE.

- USE AND THINK UPBEAT WORDS, FOR EXAMPLE 'AMAZING', 'FABULOUS', 'WONDERFUL', 'LUCKY', 'CREATIVE' ... NOTICE HOW YOUR ENERGY RISES WHEN YOU USE WORDS LIKE THIS.

- BE GLAD FOR THIS PRECIOUS DAY OF YOUR LIFE.

When her father dies Pollyanna is sent to a small town in Vermont to live with her stern and severe Aunt Polly. Well, of course Pollyanna transforms all the miserable locals (including her aunt) with her rays of sunshine, her supreme positivity and her Glad Game. It's a sentimental story for sure, but it can still bring a tear to the eye. The name Pollyanna is now part of the English language, and is used to describe overwhelming optimism. And here's the thing: cynicism never brings happiness; only optimism and appreciation can do that. Just consider those 800 Biblical references. Why not give gladness a try?

**EXERCISE:**

# Play the Glad Game

If this all seems a bit too saccharine laden for you to handle, just bear with it a bit longer. Optimism and positivity are the only barriers against unhappiness. Each time we fall into pessimism, we lose ourselves in a negative cycle and our happiness flies out of the window. *Look for happiness, focus on happiness and you will create happiness.*

Play the Glad Game for an hour. There's no need to tell anyone what you are doing. Put all your energy into seeing the good in whatever happens. If you hit a negative thought just turn it around immediately. See how you feel at the end of the Game. You might like it so much that you try it again. The Glad Game exercises those inspirational, creative and childlike parts of ourselves that we may have lost touch with in our attempt to grow up and get serious. Don't wait for your life to take off before you allow yourself to be happy; love your life and – guess what? – you will suddenly find that it *has* taken off.

## Jenny's story

Jenny is a university lecturer in sociology and loves her job. She has a wonderful family life, with one young child and an adoring and gorgeous husband (her description). And yet ... When Jenny first approached me for life coaching she was very apologetic because she said that she hadn't really got any problems; it was that she just couldn't seem to enjoy her life. Jenny felt that her happiness was always diluted by a nagging sense of worry and guilt.

This is not such an unusual state as you might think. It is entirely possible for us block our own progress and sabotage our chances if we feel that we do not really deserve the good life. Deservability is a key issue for many clients, as it was for Jenny. Because she was the eldest of five siblings, as a child Jenny had had a busy role helping her mother to look after the little ones. Her father worked hard to provide for them all and her mother (who had once been a professional pianist) devoted herself to her family.

Jenny was the only one of the children to shine academically and when she left to go to university she felt 'glad and guilty' at the same time. Her parents were very proud of her but Jenny knew that they would miss her help at home, and her three sisters were very envious of her and showed it. She had confused feelings about this chance to get ahead, even though she had created the opportunity by her own hard work. She has carried this ambivalence ever since.

Jenny needed to look back at her childhood to understand the thought patterns that were preventing her from enjoying her successes. She knew that she had made her own chances and that her siblings were free to create their own opportunities but still she felt as if she had somehow taken an unfair advantage. Eventually Jenny was able to unravel her feelings and change her deep beliefs about deserving success. As she let go of her negative beliefs she felt more and more light-hearted, joyous and free to enjoy her life.

There is little point in working towards a goal if you cannot let yourself enjoy your success when you reach it. As you take each step along the way, allow yourself to *celebrate* your successes. This not only stops you moving goalposts but it also links happiness and enjoyment with achievement. Let's face it, if going for those goals can't bring you happiness, what is the point in going for them? Remember, it's not really the goals that count but who and what you are becoming *on your way* to achieving them.

**HAPPY PEOPLE**

If you are feeling flat and worried about how your success will impact on others, check out your deservability status. Yes you *do* deserve to get the life you want. Go for it and give yourself permission to enjoy it. You are worth it!

# Celebrate!

Some people are really good at celebrating, while others find it a lot harder. It's OK if you are not the sort of person who is the life and soul of the party; quiet and solitary festivities can be just as effective as noisy sociable ones. In fact you can experience happiness every day simply by recognising that this is your chance, now, to appreciate and be glad for your life. Happiness is a feeling; all you need to do is learn how to generate it. Try any of these instant feel-goods to get you in the mood.

## 25 instant feel-goods

1  Stand up for yourself.
2  Follow your heart.
3  Make an action plan and follow it.
4  Hug a tree.
5  Treat yourself.
6  Beautify your environment.
7  Praise someone.
8  Express your true feelings.
9  Create something (a cake, a painting, a tidy room ...).
10  Tell someone how much you love them.
11  Look in the mirror and appreciate what you see.
12  Take a step towards a goal.
13  Forgive someone.

**14** Listen to your favourite music.

**15** Let yourself off the hook (you are doing your best).

**16** Know that you have a purpose.

**17** Smile, breathe and appreciate that you are alive.

**18** Have a lingering, luxuriously scented bath.

**19** Indulge in your favourite food.

**20** Laugh yourself silly.

**21** Make a daisy chain.

**22** Let the other person be right.

**23** Take some time out.

**24** Go out with your favourite friend.

**25** Write a letter to someone you love.

---

## TIME OUT

### FIVE-MINUTE RELAXATION

RELAX AND CAST YOUR MIND BACK TO WHEN YOU WERE A CHILD. ASK YOURSELF WHETHER THERE ARE ANY SPECIAL SENSUAL EXPERIENCES THAT REMIND YOU OF YOUR CHILDHOOD, FOR EXAMPLE CERTAIN SMELLS OR SONGS OR TASTES. CAN YOU REMEMBER ANY CHILDHOOD FRIENDS OR GAMES YOU USED TO PLAY? WHAT ABOUT YOUR FAVOURITE SWEETS AND OUTINGS? LET YOURSELF DRIFT BACK DOWN MEMORY LANE AND SEE WHAT YOU CAN RECALL. BECOME THAT EXCITED CHILD AT THE FAIRGROUND: SMELL THE CANDYFLOSS AND TASTE THE TOFFEE APPLES. RELIVE YOUR DELIGHT AT BEING ON THE BEACH AND PADDLING IN THE SEA. LINGER IN YOUR CHILDHOOD AND RECAPTURE SOME OF THAT MAGICAL INNOCENCE.

---

The playful and fun-loving child within you hasn't gone away; she is still there, looking for excitement and enjoyment. Your inner child is the part of you that knows how to have a good time and really get into life. Take a few moments each day to connect with her. And if she seems lost and far away (and you feel far too serious to indulge in this game) then go and do something playful - go on a swing, blow bubbles, skip, play two-ball ... The more you can connect with your inner child, the easier you will find it to enjoy and appreciate the details of your life. Let your inner child out to play from time to time and feel the difference in your mood!

And if you think you need a bit of retraining, just spend some time with a small child. It will all soon come back to you.

# Enjoy Your Work

*One way or another, we all have to find what best fosters the flowering of our humanity in this contemporary life, and dedicate ourselves to that.*

JOSEPH CAMPBELL

Recent statistics from the International Stress Management Association suggest that more than 50 per cent of the work-force believe they are affected by stress. Perhaps you are one of this majority. If you struggle to get out of bed each morning to go to a job that doesn't inspire you, then you will certainly be feeling the strain. But even if you love your job you may still be under pressure.

The phenomenon of the modern woman who is just too busy to be happy is an issue we all have to address. Satisfying and rewarding work, financial stability, a brilliant relationship, a family ... of course we want it all. But if we are to be happy we have to learn how to strike the perfect balance between these things. Flexible working hours and job share schemes may make life easier for the so-called 'time-poor' amongst us, but there are also other issues we need to look at. Many women struggle to keep their lives on an even keel. Paying the bills, having a relationship (or looking for one!) and looking after children are all time-consuming activities, and what about time for yourself? Those of you in a relationship will probably not be surprised by a recent survey that disclosed that 84 per cent of men in Britain don't do their share of the domestic chores. It's not hard to see how 'getting a life' becomes such a highly pressurised activity.

---

## QUICK TIP

STOP AND REFLECT UPON YOUR LIFE AS IT IS AT THE MOMENT. THINK ABOUT YOUR WORKING LIFE AND VISUALISE THE VERY BEST FOR YOURSELF. IMAGINE THAT YOU ARE DOING THE JOB YOU LOVE AND ARE SURROUNDED BY SUPPORTIVE COLLEAGUES.

NOW CONSIDER YOUR HOME LIFE AND CLOSE RELATIONSHIPS. PICTURE YOUR PERFECT SCENARIO. SEE YOURSELF IN A GREAT RELATIONSHIP AND LIVING IN DOMESTIC HARMONY.

NOW THINK ABOUT THE WAY YOU WOULD SPEND TIME ON YOURSELF IF YOU HAD IT, FOR EXAMPLE, SOCIALISING, MEDITATING, DANCING, READING, SWIMMING ... SEE YOURSELF DOING THE THINGS YOU WOULD LOVE TO DO IF YOU HAD THE TIME.

DON'T DWELL ON WHAT MAY APPEAR TO BE A LIFE OUT OF BALANCE (REMEMBER THAT YOU CREATE WHAT YOU THINK ABOUT). INSTEAD SPEND MOMENTS IMAGINING YOUR PREFERRED LIFESTYLE. SEE YOURSELF LOOKING RELAXED AND REFRESHED AND ENJOYING ALL ASPECTS OF YOUR LIFE AND YOU WILL START TO DRAW THIS REALITY INTO YOUR LIFE.

---

# What would you love to do?

Creating the balancing act of your life means more than putting on a good show. Even if everything is running like clockwork, if you don't like your job then your life is disastrously *out* of balance. So first things first: do you enjoy your job?

When you are doing something you love you will always have the time and the inclination for it; it will seem that you can miraculously find creative and flexible ways to fit in everything that you need to do. But if you don't like your job the pressures and stresses will soon get to you.

Clients often have lots to say about why they don't like their job but are silent when I ask them what they would love to do. Many people feel a nagging sense of dissatisfaction at work but haven't formed a clear idea of where they can best use their strengths and skills. Instead of looking *outside* at career opportunities and wondering what would suit you, why not start by looking *inside* at what excites and energises you. Discover what fascinates and motivates you, what you enjoy, what you are passionate about. Ask yourself if there is anything you would do even if you weren't paid for it? Find out what inspires you. Dare to ask yourself these big questions; dare to follow your dreams. You are special and amazing and you have come to make a unique contribution. What could it be? Where do your particular talents lie?

Answer the following questions to discover what really turns you on and gets you fired up.

- **What do you really enjoy doing?**
  Make a list of at least 20 things that give you pleasure, for example, watching Wimbledon, eating chocolate truffles, reading travel books, spending time with your family, riding your bike, swimming, going to the

ballet, having a massage, relaxing with your partner ...
Your answers will warm you up nicely for the next
question.

- **What are you passionate about?**

Whatever inspires you to jump out of bed in the
morning in an upbeat mood qualifies as a passion.
Some examples from clients include: supporting
Manchester United, playing the drums, Egyptian
dancing, using a computer, writing poetry, keeping fit,
yoga, teaching children with special needs, providing
for my family, supporting the Vegetarian Society,
running half marathons. Passion is a number of
degrees hotter than enjoyment. You know what you
*really love*. Write that list!

Rosemary Conley turned a passion into a diet and
fitness empire and has become a household name.
Her personal interest in losing weight has transformed
an £8 investment into a £13 million business which
includes exercise videos, diet books, fitness clubs,
and her own magazine and television shows.

It all began when Rosemary put on a lot of weight
while she was working as a secretary. She lost 1¹/₂
stone and fired with enthusiasm she wanted to help
others to do the same. So she booked the local village
hall and spent £8 on posters advertising her new
slimming club. She says: 'It was so exciting when
people got on the scales each week and I could tell
them that they had lost 7lb. They were thrilled. I
suddenly realised I was doing something to make
people happy. That was so rewarding.' Her classes
were so popular that she was able to leave her
secretarial job to run her slimming club, and the rest
is definitely history!

No, I know we can't all create a business empire, but this story really demonstrates the role that passion can play in giving us the confidence to get things off the ground. Think about anybody you know who really likes going to work. What do you discover? They all have one thing in common; they are *passionate* about what they do and they are using their talents and abilities to the full.

A friend of mine was a social worker for 17 years but in all that time she never really looked forward to going to work; she always dreaded Monday morning! When she hit 40 she decided enough was enough and retrained as a teacher. She is now blissfully happy in a primary school classroom where she gets to use all her creative skills every single day. I have never seen her so contented and fulfilled. The moral of this story is: you don't have to spend your whole working life doing something that doesn't inspire you. If you suffer from the Monday morning blues, you may need to rethink your career.

- **What are you good at?**

  Clients often struggle to answer this question. Don't be shy about your abilities, be proud of them. Remember that if you can't acknowledge and demonstrate your skills and strengths, no one else will ever get to know what a talented person you are. You aren't writing a CV here; this is not just about paper qualifications. Don't forget to include *everything* you are good at. What do you do best? If you are still finding this difficult, think about what you like doing; you are usually good at what you enjoy. One client, for example, answered that she was good at encouraging others, keeping optimistic most of the time, giving great parties, time management skills, entertaining small children, seeing projects through to the end and interior design. This person is obviously outgoing, sociable and supportive; she is positive and organised and can communicate well. Now look at your list and work out the qualities you demonstrate in doing what you are good at. You will discover that you have many abilities and personal strengths. Value them and use this knowledge to give you the confidence to expand your work horizons.

- **When are you in the flow?**

  You are in the creative flow when you feel buzzing, alive, focused and totally absorbed. The time just flies by because you are enjoying yourself so much. When do you feel like this? Some responses from clients include: when I am in the countryside, working on my computer, throwing pots, dancing, painting, at the gym. Take a long look at your answers. What do they tell you about your own creativity? Is there any way you can make work for yourself from any of the creative passions in your life?

Spend some time studying your answers to all four of these questions. Are you using your skills and talents to the maximum in the workplace? Have any new insights emerged that could point you in a new direction?

Or maybe you don't need to change jobs but just to take some new steps to make your working life more fulfilling and enjoyable.

IMAGINE THAT YOUR LIFE IS AN EMPTY CANVAS. YOU CAN START AFRESH AND CREATE A NEW PICTURE OF YOURSELF AND YOUR LIFE.

CHOOSE THREE PASSIONS, THREE TALENTS AND THREE PERSONAL QUALITIES THAT YOU WOULD LIKE TO SEE IN YOUR PICTURE. IMAGINE PAINTED ON YOUR CANVAS THE WORDS OR ANY SYMBOLS OR IMAGES THAT REPRESENT YOUR PASSIONS, TALENTS AND QUALITIES.

CONSIDER YOUR CHOICES. WHAT DO THEY REVEAL TO YOU?

EXERCISE:

## Your work appraisal*

Answering the following questions will help you to clarify your feelings about your job.

**1** Do you feel that your work is useful?

**2** Describe why you think it is/isn't.

**3** Do you feel valued at work?

**4** What do you like about your job?

**5** What don't you like?

**6** Are there any changes you could make to improve things.

**7** If so, why haven't you made these changes?

*Adapted from my book, *Just Do It Now!*

**8** Would you like to alter your career path?

**9** What steps could you take and why haven't you taken them?

**10** Can you imagine being happy in your job? If you can, describe what would make you happy.

Check your answers carefully. Think about the issues they reveal. What is important to you? What are your values? Does your job let you do what you believe in or do you ever feel compromised? Are you respected at work? Are your co-workers supportive and friendly? Does your team work well together? Are you in a position of authority? If so, are you able to delegate or do you carry the can for everything? Do you earn as much as you need or can you only just survive on your earnings? Would you like more responsibility?

When you are happy at work you feel valued, respected and creative, so look at exactly how you can achieve these things. If you are stuck in a job that doesn't suit you any more (or never did), take heart. People move around the workplace continually; you don't have to stay in the same place. If you need more qualifications or experience in order to change your job or get promoted, do what needs to be done. Take some careers advice and look out for courses that will give you the confidence and/or the qualifications you need to step up the career ladder. Get networking and send out copies of your CV.

Don't sit around moaning about your work, get to grips with what needs changing and then go for it. Whether you just need to change your approach (be more upbeat at work) or whether you want a brand new job the answer is the same: set some goals and get going!

# Workaholics anonymous

Workaholics are quite easy to identify once you know the symptoms. They make their lives and the lives of others miserable, so check the following characteristics to see if you are working for one or live with one or even are one yourself!

- Nothing is ever good enough
- Takes on everything that comes up
- Hates delegating
- Poor social life
- Critical and short-tempered with subordinates
- Considerable desire to please bosses
- Compulsive doer
- Can't relax
- No interest in casual chat
- Thinks and talks about work even at weekend
- Doesn't like holidays
- Loves routine
- Takes everything seriously
- Comes in early and leaves late
- Has a backlog of unused holiday time
- Always does more than is needed to do a good job
- Poor communication skills
- Lack of emotional understanding – is distant with others
- Works even when ill
- Gets things out of proportion – no sense of the bigger picture

If you are working with or for a workaholic, you will definitely be feeling stressed. If your partner is one, your home life will be affected. And if you are one, recognise the symptoms and begin to let some real life into your life. Work can be fun, creative and inspiring, but it stops being all these things if we take it too seriously.

## Bella's story

Bella is married with two children aged three and seven. She was working full-time at a local bank when she came to me for life coaching. Her husband, Mark, travelled a long way to work each day and didn't get home until about 7pm. When we first spoke, Bella was feeling very low and wanted to talk about her relationship. She said she thought she was falling 'out of love' with Mark (she had no interest in sex and found herself becoming increasingly irritated by everything he said).

But as she told me more about her life, she admitted that she was so stretched by her work and domestic commitments that

---

### QUICK TIP

ALTHOUGH IT'S TRUE THAT NO ONE CAN EVER DO A JOB IN EXACTLY THE SAME WAY AS YOU, THAT IS NO REASON TO TAKE ON THE WHOLE WORLD! DELEGATE, DELEGATE, DELEGATE. GIVE OTHERS THE CHANCE TO SHINE AND YOURSELF A CHANCE TO TAKE A BREATHER.

THINK OF THREE JOBS YOU CAN HAND OVER TO OTHERS AT HOME.

THINK OF THREE JOBS YOU CAN HAND OVER TO OTHERS AT WORK.

NOW HAND THEM OVER! DELEGATION GETS EASIER THE MORE YOU PRACTISE IT.

---

she was usually in a very negative state. She described her typical day as 'one mad dash from beginning to end'. Her day started with waking the children and getting them to nursery and school before rushing to work. Lunch times were filled with shopping, and sometimes she would even slip back home and have a clean-up. It had got to the stage where she was starting to resent both her work and her home commitments. The work at the bank got done and the work at home got done, but there was no time for anything else and certainly no time for her relationship with her husband. It's amazing how many clients come to me with a relationship problem, which, on reflection, turns out to revolve around simple lifestyle issues.

Bella had so longed to be the perfect mum and career woman that she hadn't wanted to face her true feelings before. Now she agreed that she needed some work–life balance solutions so that she could retrieve some life for herself. When she wrote down her weekly schedule it was easy to see why she was feeling depressed. She decided that her first step was to discuss the situation with her husband (instead of saying nothing and then resenting him). Bella and Mark considered their financial situation and decided they could make some cutbacks so that Bella could work part-time until the children were older. The whole thing came together very quickly, and Bella and Mark even managed to go away on a mini break to celebrate their new decision.

## Balancing work and home

You may not want to cut back your work hours (or it may not be possible), but don't let that mean you are working yourself into the ground to keep all the shows on the road.

- If you feel you are doing everything, or at least doing more than your share, at home, discuss your feelings with your loved ones. If your man is one of that 84 per cent mentioned earlier, there's talking to be done. Don't take an aggressive or blaming approach (these strategies are bound to fail). Instead point out calmly that it's not just your toilet/floor/fridge/dishes/carpet... that need cleaning or your shopping that needs doing or your dinner that needs cooking. If you feel reluctant to broach the subject, heed this warning: if you don't take a stand on household chores, you will be saddled with them forever. Alternatively, you could go halves on employing a cleaner and buy take-aways!

- If you have children make a rota of simple jobs for them to do and *stick to it*. Let them work for their pocket money. This is my cure-all for little people who make a lot of mess. If you do nothing, they will soon grow into big people who make even more mess, so train them from an early age.

- Make it your practice to leave work issues at work and home issues at home. Draw your boundaries and don't let one area of your life steal time and attention from another.

- Create a real weekend. Keep your answer machine switched on if you need to and spend quality time with your friends or loved ones.

If you are a woman who wants to have it all and you don't want to crack up in the attempt, get smart and creative and delegate. Forget about being perfect and remember that this is your life and it is here to be enjoyed! You will never stay on top of domestic chores, so why not stop trying? Relax and keep your sense of humour. There will always be floors to clean, dinners to cook, washing to do ... Get this in perspective and get some help if you need it. Slow down and take time to appreciate your wonderful life. You deserve this!

## Winning workplace strategies

When life at work starts getting to you, don't become a victim who blames her negative state on 'work stress'. You take your own mood to work, so make sure you are upbeat and friendly. Bring a positive mental approach to any workplace difficulties and always look for creative strategies to overcome problems. Your open and optimistic attitude will attract assistance and support from your co-workers and will also help to generate a pleasant working environment. And you can impress your boss without working yourself into the ground. Work smartly and creatively and solve problems rather than make them.

Try the following strategies and give your job the best shot you can. If nothing works, in spite of all your best efforts, you can take it as a sign that it's time to take your talents somewhere where they will be appreciated.

1 **Get known for your reliability**: finish tasks and get to meetings on time.
2 **Be friendly with everyone you meet** and get to know their names – others will respond positively and remember who you are.
3 **Set deadlines that are realistic**, and even overestimate the time you might need. If you get it done before the deadline you will look super-efficient.
4 **Let others know of your achievements.** Managers who know their job will be more impressed by your successes than by the hours that you put in.

5 **Look self-assured.** Fifty-five per cent of your impact comes through non-verbal communication, so make sure your body language is confident, keep a smile on your face and maintain good eye contact.

6 **Sound enthusiastic.** Look interested and be interested. Check your tone of voice on your voicemail system and if you sound a bit flat, practise until you don't.

7 **Make sure your work area is clutter-free** and have a beautiful plant or fresh flowers on your desk. The impression you give will be ordered yet creative.

8 **Remember your colleagues' birthdays** and mark them with a card and a small gift. Workplace rituals help to bring people together.

9 **Be seen as a team player** and always support others' efforts. Develop good relationships at work and the atmosphere will be much happier.

10 **Network and let people know what you are doing**. Your work contacts are the most likely gateway to promotion or a new career opportunity.

11 **Don't let awkward workmates spoil things for you.** If something needs talking through, then do it calmly and thoughtfully but let them know that you won't put up with being treated badly.

12 **Always tell others when you are impressed by them.** Even your boss will be delighted by your praise; everyone wants to feel appreciated.

13 **If you feel yourself getting angry take a deep breath** and count to 10. If that doesn't work, keep counting until it does! Never retaliate angrily in the workplace; it is very unprofessional. Calm down and then you will know the best assertive action to take.

14 **Never moan or gossip** – this leads to mistrust. Tittle-tattle always gets back to the wrong person.

15 **Keep your sense of humour!** This is probably the most important strategy of all – it can be a life-saver on a bad day and can turn a good day into a fabulous one!

---

# TIME OUT

### FIVE-MINUTE RELAXATION

CLOSE YOUR EYES AND RELAX. ALLOW YOUR BREATHING TO SLOW DOWN AND LET GO OF ANY TENSION IN YOUR BODY.

IMAGINE YOUR PERFECT JOB. SEE THE ENVIRONMENT IN AS MUCH DETAIL AS POSSIBLE. IF YOU ARE IN AN OFFICE, SEE IT AS CLEARLY AS POSSIBLE. IF YOU ARE A TEACHER, SEE THE CLASSROOM. IF YOU ARE A LANDSCAPE GARDENER, SEE THE GARDEN. IF YOU ARE A HAIRDRESSER, SEE THE SALON ... MAKE THIS FANTASY AS REAL AS YOU CAN AND PUT YOURSELF IN THE VERY CENTRE OF THE PICTURE.

DO YOU WORK ALONE OR DO YOU HAVE COLLEAGUES? WHAT TYPE OF PEOPLE ARE THEY? SEE YOURSELF TRAVELLING TO WORK. HOW DO YOU GET THERE? WHAT ARE YOU WEARING AND HOW DO YOU FEEL? WHERE DO YOU EAT LUNCH? WHO ARE YOU TALKING TO? WHAT IS THE ATMOSPHERE LIKE?

REALLY GET INTO THE SKIN OF THIS PERFECT JOB.

---

WATCH YOURSELF ENJOYING IT. FEEL YOUR HAPPINESS AND CONTENTMENT. SEE YOURSELF SMILING AND HAVING A GOOD TIME. NOTICE HOW CONFIDENT AND RELAXED YOU ARE FEELING AND HOW FRIENDLY YOUR COLLEAGUES ARE. BRING YOUR FANTASTIC DREAM JOB INTO FULL COLOUR AND HEAR THE SOUNDTRACK. *MAKE IT AS REAL AS YOU CAN!*

WHEN YOU ARE READY, OPEN YOUR EYES. REMIND YOURSELF THAT YOU ARE ONE STEP CLOSER TO YOUR PERFECT JOB, BECAUSE YOU ARE.

# Have Great Relationships

*I have to be physically attracted to someone. But I can't be with someone just because it's great sex. Because orgasms don't last long enough.*

Courtney Cox

No they don't, do they? Of course we want to fancy him like mad, but we need more than great sex in our intimate relationships; we also want friendship, love and emotional togetherness with our partner.

With statistics from the 2001 General Household Survey revealing that more than a third of 18–49-year-old women in the UK are single and that a third of these are looking to meet a long-term partner, it would seem that many women are still searching for their dream relationship. In fact the same survey states that over half of single women are optimistic that they will find the right partner some time in the next year. Of course a positive approach counts for a lot but if you can add to that some psychological understanding of relationship issues, then your chances of creating a wonderful relationship increase all the more.

'If I could only meet the perfect man I know I would feel complete.' 'If my boss was less demanding I'd have time to get out more and socialise more.' 'If my parents weren't so critical I know I'd have more confidence' … Yes, if only everyone else would get their act together, you could be in the perfect relationship! Dream on. This isn't the way it works at all.

When you look at *all* your relationships – partner, family and friends – it's tempting to think that your life would be a lot easier if only some of these people would change. But beware: if you are waiting for *anyone* to change so that your life will improve then you are acting like a victim and giving your power away. If your happiness depends on the way others act, you have lost your sense of self and none of your relationships will work. You *can* transform your present relationships and attract new and exciting friends and lovers, but you need a complete change of approach.

## What sort of relationships are you attracting?

Successful relationships begin and end with you. Do you find this hard to believe? Are you *still* trying to blame your ex for the way your relationship didn't work? Do your parents still irritate you and make you feel like a child every time you visit? Have you got friends who sometimes don't come through for you? Make a list of all the important people in your love/social/family/work life. Who on that list would you like to change? Write down exactly how you want them to change. Take a good look at this list and then throw it away. Let go of any illusion that you can change anyone's behaviour, and definitely let go of the fantasy that *if you love a man enough* you will be able change him. Men marry women and expect that they will always stay the same and women marry men thinking they can change them! We are from different planets there is no doubt. But whether you are on Mars, Venus or

Earth the same truth prevails: you can only ever change yourself. This is the magic key to creating amazing relationships.

The ways that people react towards you are a reflection of the way you feel about yourself. It works like this:

| THE WAY YOU FEEL ABOUT YOURSELF | THE WAY OTHERS REACT TO YOU |
| --- | --- |
| High in self-esteem | Respectfully |
| Angry | With hostility |
| Judgemental | Critically |
| Low in self-belief | With lack of trust |
| Positive | Responsive and receptive |
| Content and at peace | Harmoniously |
| Body confident and attractive | With interest, drawn towards you |
| Negative | Bored, unsympathetic |
| Guilty | With blame |
| Loving | Kind and caring |

If you respect yourself, others will pick up on your feelings and treat you with the respect you deserve. If you love and value yourself you will be loved and valued by others. If you think badly of yourself and are self-critical, others will reflect those feelings back to you. If you treat yourself like a victim, you will attract all the bullies in the vicinity (victims need bullies and bullies need victims). If you are low in confidence, you will soon be able to convince everyone that you are no good, useless, pathetic, etc. And if you blame yourself, well, soon enough everyone will be holding you responsible for your inadequacies.

You carry your deepest thoughts and feelings about yourself in your energy field. You don't have to say a word before others are picking up on the vibration you transmit. Check this out when you are next introduced to someone new. What 'clues' do you pick up to tell you the sort of person they are? People who are confident give off an air of authority and self-respect which you will sense even before they begin to speak. And those who struggle with issues of self-worth and self-esteem carry their negativity with them; it's very easy to spot.

Think about how you attract certain responses from the people in your life. What energy are you carrying that evokes particular reactions?

Remember that no one can 'make you' feel anything; how you feel is entirely up to you. If you really can't understand why a certain person is victimising you, ask yourself this question: why am I letting myself be treated badly? If you respect and believe in yourself, maybe its time to end this relationship.

---

## QUICK TIP

YOU CAN ONLY MAKE CHANGES IN A RELATIONSHIP WHEN YOU ARE READY TO ALTER THE MESSAGES YOU ARE SENDING TO THE OTHER PERSON. EACH TIME YOU FOCUS ON THE OTHER PERSON, YOU ARE LOOKING IN THE WRONG DIRECTION. THIS EXERCISE WILL PROVE IT. GIVE IT A TRY.

• THINK OF A TIME WHEN YOU TRIED TO CHANGE SOMEONE.

• HOW DID YOU TRY TO CHANGE THIS BEHAVIOUR?

---

- WHAT WAS THE OUTCOME?

- DESCRIBE THE SORT OF RELATIONSHIP YOU HAVE WITH THIS PERSON NOW.

- DID YOUR ATTEMPTS TO CHANGE THIS PERSON HAVE ANY EFFECT ON YOUR RELATIONSHIP? IF SO, WHAT HAPPENED?

- HAVE YOU EVER RECOGNISED A REPEATING PATTERN OF BEHAVIOUR IN YOUR RELATIONSHIPS?

- HAVE YOU EVER STAYED IN AN UNHAPPY RELATIONSHIP?

- IF SO, WHY DID YOU STAY?

- HOW DID YOU FEEL ABOUT THE OTHER PERSON INVOLVED?

- ARE YOU STILL IN THIS RELATIONSHIP?

- HOW DO YOU FEEL ABOUT YOURSELF?

THINK ABOUT YOUR ANSWERS AND LOOK TO SEE WHERE YOUR OWN FEELINGS ABOUT YOURSELF HAVE BEEN REFLECTED BACK BY SOMEONE ELSE. IF YOU VALUE AND RESPECT YOURSELF, YOU WILL ONLY HAVE RELATIONSHIPS WITH PEOPLE WHO APPRECIATE YOU. WHY WOULD YOU SPEND TIME WITH SOMEONE WHO DIDN'T?

# You are in control of your relationships

With your relationships reflecting back to you your deepest beliefs about yourself, you have the perfect training course right on your doorstep. When I work with a client on relationship issues I remind them that whatever they are going through is the exact lesson they need to learn at this time. Who needs to chase emotional and spiritual enlightenment when you have the hottest workshop in town, right here within your relationships? So how can you make the most of this reality workshop?

You create the personal realities of your life by magnetising people and circumstances into your orbit with the radiations of your own personal energy. This can be easy to accept when things are going well (your social life is buzzing, you have a wonderful new man, your family life is harmonious). When things are not so good it's more difficult to accept the responsibility for the quality of your relationships. If you and your partner are having a full-blown row it's hard to see the lesson to be learned. Who can be philosophical when their emotions are reeling? And when friendships disintegrate or a parent is annoying you, it is difficult to understand how these situations are of your own making. Why on earth would you want to attract discord into your life? When a relationship seems to be falling apart, wait until the heat dies down and then take a cool look at the personal dynamics involved. After the emotional fireworks (spoken, shouted or just felt) there will be a lull when you can re-evaluate the situation.

A client recently told me that everyone in her life seemed to be getting angry with her. When I suggested that this might be because she herself was feeling angry she denied this hotly. She said that in fact the reverse was true – that she hated displays of rage and that she made a point of never displaying her own anger. 'I'm just not an angry person,' she said.

When I asked her where she put her anger she was confused and said she just refused to accept it. But denying her anger created a build-up in her energy field and this was why she was attracting angry people wherever she turned. This client eventually accepted that she was extremely angry deep down inside and we worked with some anger management techniques that helped her to face her feelings and then to let go of them in a harmless way.

So the hottest workshop in town can teach quite subtle as well as the more obvious lessons when you are ready to learn them. Once you can accept that all your relationships are a reflection of the one you are having with yourself, you have a fabulous tool for self-development.

## EXERCISE:

# Take control

Instead of looking outside yourself and blaming others for what is lacking in your relationships, stop and answer these two important questions.

1 What is this relationship showing me about myself?
2 How can I use this insight to improve the relationships that I attract?

Dig deep and look for any repeating thought, behaviour or emotional patterns that you are experiencing. Now consider the following questions:

• Have you experienced these patterns before with this person?
• Have you ever acted out these patterns with another person?
• What does this relationship reveal to you about yourself?

- Are there any ways that you could change your patterns so that they become more positive and useful?

If you are in a poor relationship and you keep on behaving and reacting in the same ways, the relationship will stay the same. Change yourself and the relationship will change – or it will end. You are in control!

---

# TIME OUT

TRY THIS ANGER MANAGEMENT TECHNIQUE, CALLED 'SQUARE BREATHING'. USE IT WHEN YOU NEED TO CONTROL YOUR ANGER OR WHEN YOU NEED TO BRING AWARENESS AND CLARITY TO A SITUATION. IT IS A BRILLIANTLY EASY WAY TO CALM DOWN, AND NO ONE NEED KNOW WHAT YOU ARE DOING.

- INHALE SLOWLY WHILE YOU COUNT TO FIVE.

- HOLD THIS BREATH FOR A COUNT OF FIVE.

- EXHALE SLOWLY FOR A COUNT OF FIVE.

- COUNT TO FIVE BEFORE YOU BREATHE IN AGAIN.

- REPEAT THIS CYCLE A FEW TIMES.

YOU SHOULD NOW FEEL MORE COLLECTED AND IN CONTROL. USE THIS CLEAR MIND SPACE TO THINK THROUGH ANY CHOICES YOU NEED TO MAKE. WHAT DO YOU NEED TO DO TO GET THE PERSONAL OUTCOME YOU WANT?

---

# Are your relationships healthy?

*Mick and I had made this wonderful life together. That's what made the decision to divorce so difficult. It was just the infidelity that was too much ... I really did think I could change him. I thought he would settle down and be a wonderful partner, father and husband. But I had to give up.*

JERRY HALL

How much flak will you take? Exactly what will you put up with for a quiet life? Who pushes you to your limits (and sometimes beyond them)? Do you ever feel responsible for the emotions of others? When people who are close to you get angry, do you ever feel that you are to blame? Are you free to be yourself in your relationships?

As soon as you start to go for your goals and take control of your life you will find that you begin to expect more from your relationships. It's true to say that when you change yourself, your relationships will either change or end. This is because you are no longer prepared to settle for low-quality relationships that don't satisfy your needs. So don't be surprised when you find yourself re-evaluating your friendships, love life and family ties.

In psychology we refer to relationships as being 'healthy' or 'unhealthy', and you can easily work out which category each of yours falls into. A healthy relationship is one that allows you to satisfy your own basic needs. An effective way of recognising these needs is to become aware of your personal boundaries. Our boundaries are the limits we set and they reflect the distances we are prepared to go in each of our relationships. Think of this in physical terms. How much personal space do you take when you meet a stranger? Now think how physically close you get to your partner or sister or friend? Can you think of a time when a man got too familiar too soon and you felt invaded by his physical presence? This invasion of boundaries happens more subtly at the emotional level. When anyone gets too familiar or pushes you too far you will feel uncomfortable because your emotional boundaries have been invaded. Whenever you are checking boundaries the question to ask yourself is, 'How far am I prepared to go with this person?' Of course, your boundary lines will be different within each of your relationships. For example there may be things you share with your best girlfriend that you would never tell your boyfriend. Your ability to trust people may be an issue that sets the limit for you with respect to how far you can open up to others. Whatever your particular situation, you can always understand it in terms of how far you can go with anyone (physically or emotionally) *and still feel comfortable*. If you are ever uncomfortable in a relationship, you have allowed yourself to go beyond your personal boundaries.

Start to become aware of your boundaries and you will get to know who you really are, what you actually want and how much you are prepared to give. And be aware that these boundary lines can alter. After all those years of waiting for Mick to change, Jerry Hall was finally pushed to her limit. She had believed that she could change him and then finally realised that she couldn't. Looking back Jerry says, 'It was a very unhealthy relationship. I should have left him a lot earlier... I was thrilled after [the divorce] and I am getting happier every day. Now I do exactly what I want.'

Until you know your own boundaries it is impossible to

know what is right and what is wrong for you in any relationship, and you will always be full of doubt. Is it me or is it him? Is he right? Should I do what he says? Do I really want to do this or am I doing it because he wants to? What do I want? Am

I being unfair? Should I put up with this behaviour? Why am I so indecisive? If you recognise any of these feelings and have ever felt overwhelmed and taken over (particularly in an intimate relationship) just check your boundaries. Ask yourself how far you will go and then *go no further*! Remember, until you know and understand what you are worth, you cannot expect anyone else to know.

## Love is a drug

Recent research suggests that romantic attraction is a biologically based drive like sex or hunger. This helps to explain why you can fall so passionately and madly in love and behave so bizarrely in pursuit of the focus of your attention: knowing he is *the one* as soon as you meet him, staying in all night in case he rings, falling into depression when he doesn't, feeling fabulous when he just looks at you ... Love is a drug and has the power to warp the judgement of an otherwise sensible person. Scientists have discovered (as we knew all along) that we get high from falling in love. This 'lover's high' comes from a chemical called phenylethylamine (PEA), which we manufacture in our bodies when we first feel the physical sensation of romantic love. You know how wonderful this is: the whole world is rose-tinted and perfect and you feel totally and utterly wonderful! No wonder we are suckers for romance.

But the high doesn't last, and until you stop chasing it your intimate relationships will never last either. If you need this buzz to convince you that you are 'in love', you will be continually flying from one partner to the next. Romance is important but it cannot exist on its own; that initial rush of PEA will not be enough to keep your relationship going when you are cleaning the toilet and putting out the rubbish!

# Look at your Lovemap

*I've gone for each type: the rough guy; the nerdy, sweet lovable guy; and the slick guy. I don't really have a type. Men in general are a good thing.*

JENNIFER ANISTON

Well, we might wonder which category Brad Pitt falls into, hopefully none of the above if the marriage is to last! While I expect you all agree that (most of the time) men *are* a good thing, you might marvel at Jennifer's wide choice of beaux. Most of us fall repeatedly for a certain type of man, and there is a scientific reason for this.

We manufacture the love drug PEA in response to certain stimuli that turn us on at the very deepest level. When we are very young we subconsciously absorb and retain any experiences of pleasure and pain that make a powerful impression on us. This process is called sexual imprinting, and sexologist Dr John Money has created the concept of Lovemaps to describe how it works. Each of us has our own Lovemap, which holds all the positive and negative imprinting that causes us to feel sexually attracted to other people.

My friend Lorraine is always falling in and out of love. When her latest relationship (with a blonde Adonis 15 years her junior) ended, she had this to say: 'As soon as I set eyes on him I felt that wonderful excited and helpless feeling; he looked like he needed taking care of and I couldn't get him off my mind. He seemed so angelic and young with his sweet lopsided grin and long blonde hair and I knew I just had to get to know him better.' Which she did, only to discover that it takes more than a lop-sided grin to keep a relationship going. Lorraine makes a habit of falling for seemingly innocent young men who she thinks only need the love of a good woman (her) to turn them into the man of her dreams. She loves falling in love and when it inevitably ends (they are never innocent enough!) she goes out and does it all over again.

If a certain look or smile or hairstyle can turn you into a quivering jelly at the sight of a stranger, recognise that you do this. Enjoy the buzz for what it is but don't expect it to lead to wedded bliss; it won't! 'Hopeless' and 'helpless' are words we often use to describe our feelings when we are high on PEA, but in the cold light of day you know these are not adjectives that you really want to describe you. Don't get me wrong. I adore love and romance, but I also know that we all have to go beyond our sexual imprinting if we are ever to have a great relationship.

**EXERCISE:**

# Your Lovemap*

1 What physical features do you usually fall for?

2 How would you describe the type of person that most attracts you?

3 Which qualities do your past lovers share (positive and negative)?

4 Would you say that you always go for the same type?

5 Does this type suit you?

6 Do relationships with your favourite type often end in tears?

*Adapted from my book, *Be Yourself*

Positive imprintings are easy to recognise. Perhaps your father was a keen sportsman and you now find yourself attracted to sporty men; maybe your elder brother had a floppy fringe and now you are besotted with anyone with a foppish Hugh Grant hairstyle. Such attractions are not harmful, unless of course they are the only ones that hold the relationship together.

But our Lovemaps can also be negative, and it is these imprintings that can cause us to make poor relationship decisions. Guided by our sexual imprinting we can find ourselves in an inappropriate relationship time and time again. It is even possible for us to become addicted to people with behaviour patterns that are critical or abusive. A surprising number of clients tell me that they always seem to be attracted to men who can't show their feelings. When I pursue this with them they often reveal that their own father was emotionally distant when they were growing up. Think about your own Lovemap and look particularly for any repeating patterns that don't seem to work for you. If you find yourself caught in a compulsive attraction for a person who is not good for you, then recognise the relationship for what it is. Avoid the attraction traps that cause you emotional pain and try a different 'type' entirely. You will attract whoever you think you deserve. You can choose who to love.

## Create positive relationships

You are in control of all your relationships so don't blame anyone else for the things that go wrong in them. Whether you are looking at your friendships, your family connections or your love life, always bear in mind that you are experiencing the sort of relationships you are experiencing because you are attracting them. If you are going for your dreams and taking control of your life you will know the value of positive and optimistic people who believe in you. Such people are called your 'believing mirrors' because they reflect back to you your own self-belief and confidence. Who is it that cheers you on and says, 'Yes go for it' or 'You can do it'? Who is always there for you, to listen to your problems and to encourage you when you are feeling down? Who amongst your friends, relations and lovers act as believing mirrors for you? These are the people who know how to have a meaningful and complete relationship with you because they want the best for you. Sometimes we can find ourselves taking these valuable people for granted while we chase after the good opinion of others who we might be trying to impress or please in some way. The golden rules for relationship are:

- Cultivate positive relationships with everyone and always recognise the people who are there for you through thick and thin.
- Choose your friends carefully.
- Maintain any difficult family relationships with diplomacy and tact.
- Check that your lover has all the qualities you are looking for (and not just a sexy pair of blue eyes!).

## TIME OUT

### FIVE-MINUTE RELAXATION

CLOSE YOUR EYES, RELAX AND BECOME AWARE OF YOUR BREATHING. LET ALL THOUGHTS DRIFT AWAY AS YOU FOCUS ON THIS VISUALISATION.

- **Imagine** yourself at the centre of a circle of people.

- **You** recognise everyone in the circle as someone who is or has been very close to you. Let your circle include family, lovers and close friends. This is your circle of love, and everyone in it has come into your life to teach you something of great significance about yourself.

- **Look** at each one in turn and ask yourself, 'What gift did this person bring me?'

- **Let** each person step forward one at a time and give you their gift.

- **It** doesn't matter if you don't know what it is. Just take what they hand you, smile and thank them.

- **When** all the gifts are at your feet, dissolve the circle and come out of the visualisation.

**You** may already have recognised some, many or none of your gifts, but eventually you will recognise them all. Remember that not all gifts come gift-wrapped! Some come in disguise as problems or challenges, and they offer you the unique opportunity to develop your strength in overcoming them.

**Be** thankful to everyone for the gifts they bring.

# Grow Rich

*I don't know much about being
a millionaire, but I'll bet I'd be
darling at it.*

DOROTHY PARKER

Yes, we understand that money can't buy happiness/love/ peace etc. but we would all like the chance to find out what sort of millionaires we would make. Let's start the ball rolling by imagining how it would feel to be rich. What would wealth bring you that you haven't got already? How different would you feel if you had lots of cash in the bank? Hold that feeling!

And now let's turn to the magical power of positive thought. Expect success and you will get it, expect to feel rich and prosperous and you will, expect money and it will materialise it.

Jim Carrey is a positive thinker who has used all the principles that you have read about in *Weekend Life Coach* to create a fabulous career and earn lots of money. He firmly believes that, '... you manifest what you think in this world'. In the days when he was struggling to make his name he wrote himself a cheque for $7 million; it was his way of visualising himself as being 'in with the top guys'. It was his dream to make it to the top and he says that he still dreams about it. He persistently believed that he would succeed and he fully expected to receive cheques paying him millions of dollars. As he earned about $20 million from his last movie we are clearly looking at a man who knows the power of creative visualisation.

Although making it big in Hollywood may not be our personal dream, we can always learn a trick or two from someone who has become successful.

You are always in the process of creating your own reality with the power of your beliefs and you know that you attract whatever you keep thinking about. If you focus on scarcity and lack, this is what you will attract. And if you think and act as if you are poor and impoverished, you will continue to be so.

## The meaning of prosperity

Prosperous (adj.) 1 flourishing; prospering. 2 rich; affluent; wealthy. 3 favourable or promising.

COLLINS ENGLISH DICTIONARY

I love the word 'prosperous'. It sounds so full of promise and wellbeing. Are you feeling prosperous? Prosperity doesn't depend on large deposits in the bank. A person can be rich in money but poor in the things that really matter. Consider these two people. One has lots of money but is insecure about how to keep it, afraid of theft and feels guilty about her wealth. The other has much less money but loves her life and knows how to enjoy what she has. Who is richer in the resources of life? Who feels more prosperous? If you feel rich in the good things of life they will be attracted to you.

I once had a famous and very wealthy client who spent most of her time trying to hide away from the spotlight (except when she was publicising her latest venture). She came to me to help her solve what she called her 'pile of relationship problems'. And she did indeed have a pile! Celebrity status and all that goes with it looks so glamorous and ritzy, and who amongst us hasn't wished to mix and mingle with the gloriously rich and famous? But there can be a downside if you don't have a close circle of friends who can keep secrets and share the trials and tribulations that the lifestyle inevitably brings. My client had risen from rags to riches very quickly and this had caused all sorts of problems in her social life. Her parents were overawed by her success and her wealth and this had at first created a huge rift. Her relationship with her brother and sister had become a lot less close and she said that they always seemed a bit suspicious of her. And when a past boyfriend revealed a tasty titbit from her past to one of the tabloids she felt over-exposed and vulnerable. She had lost all her trust in people and this was where she was at when I met her.

Eventually she withdrew from her old friends and started to see less of her family. In time she built up a new social circle that she could trust, and only when she felt stronger did she start to see her family again. By this time everyone had got more used to her fame and glory. Those old relationships smoothed out a bit but were never the same as they used to be.

Why have I told you this story? No, it's not meant to preach the perils of celebrity success but to demonstrate that money in itself doesn't necessarily bring the flourishing, favourable and promising rewards of prosperity.

## Rich energy and poor energy

When you are feeling prosperous you are positive, generous and upbeat, and you radiate feelings of trust, open-heartedness and abundance. What is it that brings you this personal sense of satisfaction? Are you rich in friendships, love, health, awareness, success, abilities, interests ...?

Prosperity consciousness surrounds you with 'rich energy', which attracts even more positive outcomes (you attract whatever you radiate). Appreciate all that you have and recognise the abundance of good things in the universe, and every aspect of your life will dramatically improve.

If you are experiencing any deficiency in your life it's only too easy to blame it on lack of money. But think again. You know that money can't buy the qualities that bring you happiness. If you feel impoverished it is because you are not getting enough of what you want, whether it's love, attention, success, confidence, money or whatever. What is it that you feel you lack? Scarcity consciousness and a negative fear-based outlook will create an aura of 'poor energy' around you and this will attract a sense of shortage and lack into every corner of your life (including your finances). Change your 'poor energy' to 'rich energy' by affirming prosperity consciousness instead of scarcity consciousness.

Whenever you feel a sense of lack and scarcity in your life, repeat some of the prosperity affirmations in column A of the table below*. They will lift your energy and change your mood. Don't get stuck in a negative worldview that makes you a depressed victim of a system that you cannot change. Back hope instead of hopelessness, go for beliefs that make you feel good, affirm prosperity and it will be yours. Expand your vision, embrace the benevolent energy of the universe and let abundance flow into your life.

| A<br>**AFFIRMATIONS OF PROSPERITY**<br>*I believe that* | B<br>**AFFIRMATIONS OF SCARCITY**<br>*I believe that* |
| --- | --- |
| The more I give the more I get. | The more I give the less I have. |
| Life is a celebration. | Life is a disappointment. |
| We are here to take care of each other. | Everyone is alone. |
| I can change my reality. | I am a victim of circumstance. |
| There is always enough of everything to go round. | Our resources are running out. |
| Scarcity is only an idea that we have created. | Scarcity exists; it is the only reality. |
| We are all connected. | I am insignificant in the grand scheme of things. |
| My beliefs create the quality of my life. | Events are outside my control. |

*Adapted from my book, *The Self-Esteem Workbook*

Do you live in a frightening world or an abundant universe? Which way of looking at things gives hope and power and which ensures that you stay a victim? Yes, it is true that vital resources are running out, our seas are being poisoned, there are holes in the ozone layer and people are starving and dying in wars. Things are like this, but why are they? There is a mass belief that *there will never be enough of anything to go round* and so we must be forever fighting for scarce resources and competing for our survival. But we have created this idea of scarcity from our own fears and feelings of lack. Scarcity is an idea that becomes a reality if we believe in it, so *don't buy into it!* The universe is abundant; it has everything we need. If we co-operate with nature and with each other we will have ample resources. Just think what would happen if our world governments abounded in abundance awareness. We could all prosper and flourish!

## Attract more money

To those of you would like to attract more money I say this: start, as always, with your beliefs. This is how you create your reality.

If you worry about money you will find yourself in a downward spiral of poverty and deprivation. When you send out negative messages ('I have no money,' 'I am poor,' 'I can't pay the bills' ...) your unconscious will support your beliefs and keep manifesting this reality for you. You will get more of what you are affirming, and in this case that means less and less money.

So check your money beliefs. What are your thoughts drawing into your life? Your deep beliefs about money can make or break you financially. For example if your thought

# QUICK TIP

REPEAT THIS AFFIRMATION: *THE ABUNDANCE OF THE UNIVERSE IS MINE.*

IF YOU REALLY DON'T BELIEVE IT, THEN YOU WILL NEED TO KEEP ON REPEATING IT. LET THOSE SCARCITY BELIEFS GO. THEY WILL KEEP YOU POOR IN EVERYTHING, INCLUDING MONEY. START LOOKING FOR ABUNDANCE WHEREVER YOU GO. YOU WILL FIND THAT THERE IS JUST SO MUCH OF EVERYTHING.

- LOOK AT THAT TOMATO YOU ARE HAVING FOR LUNCH. HOW MANY SEEDS ARE INSIDE?

- HOW LOVING CAN YOU BE? HOW MUCH LOVE DO YOU HAVE IN YOUR HEART? YOU ARE FULL OF LOVE; THERE IS NO SHORTAGE.

- THE OAK TREE PRODUCES ENOUGH ACORNS TO ENSURE THAT WE WILL NEVER BE SHORT OF OAK TREES (UNLESS WE CUT THEM ALL DOWN OF COURSE).

- AND HOW ABOUT TADPOLES IN THE POND? THOSE FROGS JUST KEEP ON COMING.

FOCUS ON ABUNDANCE AND YOU WILL FIND IT *EVERYWHERE.*

was that money is unclean or that it might compromise you in some way, it's unlikely that you will ever be able to let it flow into your life; you would be too worried about its bad influence. If at some level you don't believe you deserve much, you will always stay trapped in your 'poor energy' (receiving only as much as you think you deserve). Those who have an easy relationship with money can love it and accept it with no negative emotions attached. Money flows easily to such people. So let go of money worries unless you want to stay poor. And instead of worrying about being poor and asking yourself 'What will I do without enough money?', get creative and ask yourself 'What can I do to create more money?'

Take a look at the real state of your finances, check your spending and saving habits, plug any money drains and you will immediately find yourself feeling more empowered and in control of the money in your life.

## Money, sex and shopping

With marriage failure rates currently running at an all time high of 40 per cent, and with arguments about money and sex often cited as the main causes of partnership break-up, here is yet another good reason to clarify your financial situation.

For most of us, our relationship with money is like our relationship with sex and food; it's complex and overlaid with strong emotions. And money is like sex and food, in the sense that when we don't have enough of it we can't stop thinking about it, and when we do have enough of it we have the time and energy to think about other things! Can we ever have enough of money? Have you got enough? Do you want more? How do you think your life would improve if you were richer? Can you resist those stunning stilettos that would be so perfect on you? Are you out on the town spending money like Posh and Becks as soon as pay day arrives? Are you in debt? Take heart if you are. A major money survey commissioned by a top UK magazine has revealed that the average debt is around

£2,000 (and 10 per cent of participants owe this on credit cards alone, as well as having bank loans and overdrafts), so you are certainly not on your own if you are spending beyond your means!

High priestess of feminism Germaine Greer tells us that 'A woman is always equipped for shopping, in case some window of opportunity should open in her busy day.' And although she is being ironic here, she is probably right; most of us love a spot of retail therapy, and why not? Sometimes we might be tempted to splash out on a must-have item; well a girl's got to go mad sometimes! But if this becomes a habit we can soon find ourselves with mounting debts.

Spending and lifestyle experts define two types of extravagance. The first type is designed to show off, while the second, and more common, type is kept strictly secret. If you have ever hidden new clothes in the back of the wardrobe and/or lied about the price of a new purchase, then you know about this second type. Oh, let's face it, we have all made secretly extravagant buys, and I'm quite sure that they are very good for our morale, *as long as we can afford them*. And there's the snag! If you love shopping and you can afford what you buy, then go on, indulge! But if you are not managing your debts, your spending habits need reviewing.

## Keep a money diary

If you have good financial habits, you will be in full knowledge of the details of your income and expenditure and you will be one of a tiny minority. For the rest of you 'natural spenders', who love to shop until you drop and haven't much of a clue about the state of your bank balance from week to week, there is only one way forward: to create a money diary.

# Your spending/saving habits

Answer the following questions and see what they reveal.

1 Do you spend more than you earn?

2 Would you describe yourself as a natural saver or a natural spender? Or are you somewhere in the middle?

3 Are you an impulse buyer?

4 What is the biggest impulse buy you have ever made?

5 Have you any savings? If so, how much?

6 Do you work to a budget?

7 What percentage of your income do you think you need to save? Are you saving this amount?

8 Are you ever in denial over your financial affairs (bills unopened, unrealistic attitude to the costs of living, etc.)?

9 List ten unrewarding ways that you have spent money this month.

10 Think of three things you can do to reduce your expenditure. If you need to, do them!

---

This will not be as terrifying as you think; in fact it will be a revelation. Whenever I work with clients to improve their financial situation they always panic at the thought of getting their spending habits down in black and white. But every one of them has found it to be an empowering experience.

Write down *every single item* of expenditure for a week and leave nothing out, for example: Tube fares, drinks in the pub, M&S knickers, coffees, crisps, Philip Treacy hat, Maltesers, lip gloss, food shopping ... *everything* you buy. At the end of the week draw your own conclusions. One client stopped her expensive daily cappuccino habit and could afford a night out at the theatre at the end of the month. You will be surprised to discover how your money is just dribbling away on bits and pieces; you don't have to be a shopaholic to spend more than you earn.

When you have recovered from the shock, continue with the diary until you have a month's worth of entries. Check your out-goings against the money you have left after your essential bills have been paid.

OK, now you know what is really going on and you can start to take control of the situation.

## 10 instant money savers

1 As you stand in front of the shop window and experience that must-have urge, stop and count to 10 slowly. Then ask yourself, 'Do I really need this?' And if you are still blinded by desire, ask yourself, 'Can I afford this?' Both cruel questions, I know, but they are also critical questions. Get into this good shopping habit: interrupt your longing with cool logic. Just think how much this will have saved you by the end of the month!

2 Instead of eating out with your friends why not have them round to your place for a simple meal, and let them bring the wine and pudding.

3 Wait until the sales to do your clothes shopping. You will get some great bargains (and feel really virtuous instead of guilty).

4 Resist hire purchase agreements (very costly). It's worth saving up for that big item until you can pay for it with cash. You will pay far less.

5 Have a hunt around your local charity shops and you may well find a designer bargain. Check out upmarket second-hand 'nearly new' shops that sell designer clothes for a fraction of their original cost.

6 Eat a good meal before you go food shopping. Supermarkets employ numerous 'visual merchandising' tricks to tempt you to fill that trolley and you have far more chance of resisting if you aren't hungry when you get there. And while you are there, keep an eye open for Bogofs, as in Buy One Get One Free. These are good money-saving deals as long as you make sure you are getting two of something that you were going to buy anyway.

7 If you are spending £5 a day on lunch and drinks, that adds up to £100 a month. Take your own lunch to work and you will save over half of what you were spending. Just think how much this will amount to over a year.

8 Work out your budget for daily expenditure and stick to it! This doesn't have to make life unexciting and dull. Work out how much you will save by stopping impulsive buys and save it! Then you will be able to afford that big item (such as a holiday). Now that is worth waiting for!

9 Join a library and order the books you would otherwise have to buy. Check out the DVDs, CDs and videos too.

10 Save regularly and treat this as an essential payment. Set up a direct debit and then you can forget all about it and it will accumulate nicely!

# Set your financial goals

As soon as you become aware of your money habits (spending, saving and squandering) you can take immediate positive steps towards having more money. Set some financial goals for yourself and don't expect too much too soon or you might be tempted to blow all your good intentions. Some realistic and useful short-term goals might include: to keep a money diary, to stick to a realistic budget, to stop impulse buying and to work on increasing your feelings of prosperity. Your long-term goals might be to take financial advice, increase your earnings, save for a big item and become more relaxed about money issues.

Don't ever forget that the key to your prosperity lies in your attitude. Think rich, let go of worries and negative beliefs about money and welcome feelings of abundance into your life. Work on your positive beliefs and step out of scarcity consciousness. As soon as you do this you will find that you will want to get to grips with the ins and outs of your financial affairs. Take control of your money issues, believe that you deserve to be rich and you will open the door to a life of abundance and prosperity. You are worth it!

# TIME OUT

## FIVE-MINUTE RELAXATION

YOU ARE AMAZING. I WONDER IF YOU ARE FEELING IT RIGHT NOW. CLOSE YOUR EYES AND DO SOME DEEP AND RELAXING BREATHING.

- START TO THINK ABOUT WHAT A WONDERFUL PERSON YOU ARE.

- NOW IMAGINE MEETING A FRIEND WHO TELLS YOU SOMETHING THAT THEY REALLY LIKE ABOUT YOU. SEE THIS PERSON SMILING AND APPRECIATING YOU.

- NOW HERE COME SOME MORE PEOPLE, AND THEY ARE AGREEING THAT YOU ARE INDEED A VERY AMAZING PERSON.

- IGNORE ANY FEELINGS OF EMBARRASSMENT AND JUST KEEP GOING.

- A CROWD OF PEOPLE IS ARRIVING. THEY CLUSTER AROUND YOU SHOWING THEIR LOVE AND APPRECIATION.

- NOW YOU ARE ON A STAGE AND THE WHOLE AUDIENCE IS CLAPPING AND CHEERING AND APPRECIATING YOU. HEAR THE APPLAUSE AND FEEL THE LOVE AND RESPECT OF ALL THESE PEOPLE. SMILE AND TAKE A BOW. YES, YOU DESERVE THIS LEVEL OF SUPPORT AND APPRECIATION.

YOU REALLY ARE FABULOUS AND SPECIAL. FEEL IT NOW!

# Epilogue
# You Are Amazing

*If you don't tell the truth about yourself,*
*you cannot tell it about other people.*

VIRGINIA WOOLF

You are amazing! This is the truth about you, so go out there and tell it, feel it and live it. The woman who smiles back at you from the mirror knows her true worth and she expresses it in every moment of her life.

Love her for her grit and determination, her resilience in the face of sometimes overwhelming odds. Admire her style and grace when the chips are down and she is negotiating her future. Respect her flexibility and creativity as she hurdles her challenges and goes on to win the obstacle race. Comfort her when she is down and marvel at the way she rises up and bounces back yet again! No, you can't keep a good woman down; she is always moving onwards and upwards in pursuit of her dreams.

I know that you have the energy and willpower to push towards your goals, and this sense of direction and purpose will make you feel like a winner every time. What more can you ever do than have a go and do your best? And when things don't always turn out the way you had hoped, you are safe and secure in the knowledge that you gave it your best shot; this is what is meant by a winning mentality. Let nothing grind you down. Let no one diminish you. Believe in yourself and know that you are here to do great things, so get out there and do them!

You have come bearing gifts; use them well. Appreciate the miracle of who you are and what you are becoming and learn to love your life; this is really the greatest thing that you can do. Take your love and laughter out into the world and you will make a huge difference to everyone you meet. Touch others with your enthusiasm and boundless optimism. Positive energy is the greatest gift you can share with anyone.

*Weekend Life Coach* has been such fun to write and I hope that it has inspired you to take the next exciting step of your journey. If you would like to get in touch with me or find out more about my life-coaching services just go to

www.weekendlifecoach.com

or email me at
lyndafield@weekendlifecoach.com

I look forward to hearing from you.

With all my best wishes

*Lynda Field*

# References and Inspirational Books

Cameron, Julia, *Walking in this World*, Rider, 2002

Carlson, Richard, *Don't Sweat the Small Stuff*, Hodder and Stoughton, 1998

Field, Lynda, *Creating Self-Esteem,* Vermilion, 2001
—*The Self-Esteem Workbook*, Vermilion, 2001
—*Just Do it Now,* Vermilion, 2001
—*365 Inspirations for a Great Life*, Vermilion, 2002
—*Be Yourself*, Vermilion, 2003

Hanh, Thich Nhat, *Peace is Every Step,* Rider, 1995

Hay, Louise, *You Can Heal Your Life*, Eden Grove Editions, 1988

Hill, Napoleon, *Think and Grow Rich*, Ballantine Books, 1983

Kabat-Zinn, Jon, *Mindfulness Meditation for Everyday Life*, Piatkus, 1994

McKenna, Paul, *The Hypnotic World of Paul McKenna*, Faber and Faber, 1993

Peale, Norman Vincent, *You Can If You Think You Can*, Cedar Books, 1974

Pearson, Allison, *I Don't Know How She Does It*, Vintage, 2003

Pegg, Mike, *The Positive Workbook,* Enhance, 1995

Roman, Sanaya, *Personal Power Through Awareness*, H.J. Kramer, Inc., 1989

Schaef, Anne Wilson, *Meditations for Women Who do too Much*, Harper Collins, 1996

Wiseman, Richard, *The Luck Factor*, Century, 2003

# Index

## Win a Personalised Life Coaching Course with the UK's Leading Personal Growth Expert Lynda Field

Enter our Weekend Life Coach Free Prize Draw to win a face-to-face, personal consultation with Lynda Field and three weekly coaching sessions via phone or email – depending on your preference.

Just send your name, address, telephone number and email address (optional) on a postcard to:

Weekend Life Coach Prize Draw,
Ebury Press Marketing Department, PO Box 4313,
20 Vauxhall Bridge Road, London SW1V 2SA

by 31st March 2004.

### Terms and Conditions

The first entry to be drawn will be declared the winner.

The draw will take place on April 15th 2004.

The winner will be notified by April 30th 2004.

No employees from The Random House Group Ltd or participating retailers may enter.

Entries only accepted from within the UK.

No purchase necessary.

The judge's decision is final and no correspondence will be entered into.

It is a condition of entry that the winner agrees to the use of their name, address and photograph in publicity material. However, we will not archive, or utilise any entrant's name or address for anything unrelated to this competition.

No cash alternative.

Prize does not include transport or any additional expenses.

The promoter is The Random House Group Ltd, 20 Vauxhall Bridge Road, London SW1V 2SA.